Practical Strategies for Applied Budgeting and Fiscal Administration

Practical Strategies for Applied Budgeting and Fiscal Administration

What Works for P-12 Administrators

Spencer C. Weiler and Gabriel R. Serna

ROWMAN & LITTLEFIELD
Lanham • Boulder • New York • London

Published in partnership with the
Association of School Business Officials International

Published by Rowman & Littlefield
A wholly owned subsidiary of The Rowman & Littlefield Publishing Group, Inc.
4501 Forbes Boulevard, Suite 200, Lanham, Maryland 20706
www.rowman.com

Unit A, Whitacre Mews, 26-34 Stannary Street, London SE11 4AB

British Library Cataloguing in Publication Information Available

Library of Congress Cataloging-in-Publication Data
Names: Weiler, Spencer, author. | Serna, Gabriel Ramon, author.
Title: Practical strategies for applied budgeting and fiscal administration : what works for P-12 administrators / Spencer C. Weiler and Gabriel R. Serna.
Description: Lanham, Maryland : Rowman & Littlefield, 2016. | Includes bibliographical references.
Identifiers: LCCN 2016014004 | ISBN 9781475825640 (cloth : alk. paper) | ISBN 9781475825657 (pbk. : alk. paper) | ISBN 9781475825664 (electronic)
Subjects: LCSH: School budgets—United States. | Public schools—United States—Business management. | Public schools—United States—Finance.
Classification: LCC LB2830.2.W45 2016 | DDC 371.2/06—dc23
LC record available at https://lccn.loc.gov/2016014004

♾ ™ The paper used in this publication meets the minimum requirements of American National Standard for Information Sciences—Permanence of Paper for Printed Library Materials, ANSI/NISO Z39.48-1992.

Printed in the United States of America

It is often said that in order for people to succeed they must have key figures that provide them support at pivotal points in life. I have been incredibly blessed to have people surface in my life, who have instilled in me a vision of myself that I could not see at the time. There are three people in particular I would like to dedicate this book to:

Stan Seaberg—A high school history teacher who showed me the joy of learning
Tom Taylor—A dear friend who pushed me physically and intellectually
David D. Williams—A mentor and close friend who encouraged me to grow as an educator, researcher, and scholar

—Spencer's

For my beautiful mother, Mary
—Gabriel's

Contents

Foreword   xiii

Acknowledgments   xv

1 The Importance of Money in Public Education   1
    The Importance of Money   2
    The Importance of Budget Management Skills   2
    The Book's Organization   4
    Parting Thoughts before the Fun Begins   4
    Guiding Questions   5
    Additional Reading   5
    Exercises   6

PHASE I: FOUNDATION   7

2 Getting to Know a Budget   9
    Why Budgets?   10
    P-12 Budget: The Purpose   10
    Allocating Budget Funds   12
        Student-Based Budgeting   12
        Zero-Based Budgeting   13
        Incremental Budgeting   14
        Budget Hybrids in P-12   14
    Major Budgeting Categories   15
        P-12 Budgeting: Revenue   15
        P-12 Budgeting: Allocation   16
        Operating and Capital Budgets: Basic Difference   17
    Philosophy of Budget Management   18

Conclusion   19
Guiding Questions   20
Additional Reading   20
Exercises   21

3 Anticipating Revenues and Expenditures   **23**
What Are Revenues?   23
Revenues for P-12   24
   The Origins of P-12 Revenues   24
   P-12 Revenues from a School District's Perspective   26
   Voter-Approved Mill Levy Override   26
Accurately Forecasting and Forecasting Accuracy   28
Expenditures and Costs   29
   Definitions of Typical Costs in Education   29
   P-12: Expenditures   30
Cost–Benefit Analysis   34
Accurately Forecasting and Forecasting Accuracy:
      Cost Considerations   35
Conclusion   36
Guiding Questions   36
Additional Reading   37
Exercises   37

4 Basics of Financial Ratio Analysis   **43**
Financial Ratios   43
   Uses of Financial Ratios   44
Types and Interpretation of Financial Ratios   45
   Liquidity Ratios   45
   Operating Performance Ratios   47
   Debt and Solvency Ratios   50
   Source Ratios   52
Cautions on Financial Ratio Analysis   53
Conclusion   53
Guiding Questions   53
Additional Reading   54
Exercises   54

5 Forecasting, Accuracy, and Judgment   **57**
Expectations and Uses of Forecasting Results   58
Forecasting Approaches and Methods   58
   Using Averages for Forecasting   59
   Exponential Smoothing   62
   Correlation Analysis   63
   Using Linear Models and Regression for Forecasting   65

Regression Forecasting   65
Curvilinear Models: A Brief Overview   68
Judgment in Forecasting   69
Conclusion   72
Guiding Questions   72
Additional Reading   72
Exercises   73

**PHASE II: DEVELOPING AND OVERSEEING
THE TOTAL PROGRAM**   **77**

6   The Budget Cycle   **79**
Budgeting in Periods of Economic Growth   80
  Specific Points to Consider When Creating a P-12 Budget
    during Periods of Economic Growth   80
Budgeting in Periods of Economic Reduction   81
  Specific Strategies to Consider When Creating a P-12 Budget
    during Periods of Economic Reduction   82
The P-12 Budget Cycle   83
Conclusion   86
Guiding Questions   86
Additional Reading   86
Exercises   87

7   Oversight and Budget Variance Analysis   **89**
Variances in Revenues and Expenditures   89
Oversight and the Role of Cyclical and Structural Variances   90
Variance Analysis Using Summary Measures   91
  Standard Error of Estimate   92
  Mean Absolute Deviation   94
  Mean Squared Error   96
  Mean Absolute Percentage Error   96
Approach for Oversight and Monitoring of Forecast Variance   98
  Control Chart   98
Audit, Accountability, and Transparency   101
Conclusion   103
Guiding Questions   103
Additional Reading   103
Exercises   103

PHASE III: CAPITAL PROJECTS WITH AND WITHOUT DEBT   107

8   Capital Budgets without Debt   **109**
Funding New Projects without Debt   112

Capital Fund-Raising and Campaigns   112
Paygo and Usage of Fund Balances   113
Time Value of Money   114
Discounting and Compounding Basics   115
Annual Cash Flows and Choosing Projects   117
Present Values with Annual Costs   120
Net Present Value and Cash Flows   123
Choosing the Discount Rate   125
Conclusion   126
Guiding Questions   126
Additional Reading   126
Exercises   127

9   Capital Budgeting and Debt   **131**
What Is Bonding?   131
Why Use Debt?   132
Credit Ratings and Factors Related to Bond Rates   132
Credit Rating Symbols and Qualifiers   133
Ratings, Debt Service, and the Total Program   134
Associated Rating Factors   134
Actors in the Bond Process and Steps for Issuing Debt   136
Actors in a Bond Issue   136
Steps in a Bond Issue   137
Conclusion   137
Guiding Questions   139
Additional Reading   139
Exercises   139

PHASE IV: LINKAGE, PHILOSOPHY, AND CONCLUSION   **141**

10 Budget Alignment with Strategic Plan   143
Guiding Principles within an Organization   143
Misalignment Examples   144
Misalignment Example #1   145
Misalignment Example #2   146
Final Thoughts Related to Misalignment   147
Revisiting Mission, Vision, Goals, and Strategic Plan   147
Analyzing Spending Patterns   148
Correcting Spending Patterns   149
Conclusion   149
Guiding Questions   150
Additional Reading   150
Exercises   150

11 Conclusion 153
Know Who to Ask 154
Alignment 154
Transparency 154
Collaborate 155
Educate Others 155
Use Knowledge to Influence Others 155

References 157

About the Authors 163

Foreword

Professors Spencer Weiler and Gabriel Serna have prepared a very useful and informative resource for those who are entrusted with administering funds allocated to finance public elementary and secondary schools. Both experienced professionals and those developing skills necessary to successfully manage the fiscal resources provided to sustain the American common schools will find this work to be a valuable asset.

This book, *Practical Strategies for Applied Budgeting and Fiscal Administration: What Works for P-12 Administrators*, is not a theoretical treatise; instead, it is a set of proven and practical methods that the authors believe will be helpful to those who are, or will be, assigned the responsibility of administering public funds for the education of the nation's youth. The authors did not give in to the temptation to describe primarily the budgetary processes of their home states and localities. Rather, their development of *practical strategies* was based on examples drawn from various states, or from the nation as a whole.

Readers will also find that the authors include a refreshing complaint throughout their work; they point to the problem of *educational equity*, or the lack of fiscal equity among states, and certainly among school districts within almost all states. More distressingly, they suggest that per pupil fiscal disparities continue to increase.

In the first chapters, the authors assume that the readers are not experienced finance or budget officers, and they begin with an introduction to the basics, that is, explanation of terms such as revenue, expenditure, and so on. They quickly bring the readers *up to speed* and delve into the primary purpose of their work in the next series of chapters, that is, the sharing of *practical strategies of budgeting*. They present a series of discussions concerning budget cycles, budget oversights and controls, audits, and statistical analyses.

While the authors primarily focus on the current operation of public schools, they also thoroughly address the acquisition and financing of capital facilities and the management of long-term debt. Although many school budget officers are not involved with the administration of capital facilities or the management of long-term debt, those who are so charged will find these discussions both relevant and useful.

Throughout the book, each chapter includes a series of interesting questions that have been designed to stimulate class discussions and to challenge readers. The book has been well crafted and is very insightful, and the title, *Practical Strategies for Applied Budgeting*, aptly describes its purpose and content. It should serve well as a primary text for graduate classes in the areas of School Business Management and Public School Budgeting. It also should prove useful as an ancillary text for graduate classes in Public School Finance, where the purposes are twofold: (1) provision of a theoretical basis for the financing of public schools; and (2) provision of an introductory set of skills necessary to administer school budgets.

Richard G. Salmon
Professor Emeritus
Virginia Tech

Acknowledgments

We wish to express our appreciation to a number of people who have helped out immensely as this book slowly morphed from an idea to a reality. Luke Cornelius and Carlee Escue-Simon were instrumental in initiating this project and provided the original vision for the niche the book might be able to fill. In addition, we would like to thank the HESA 696 class at the University of Northern Colorado for testing chapter materials and providing wonderful feedback; especially Andrea DeCosmo, who passed a careful eye over our equations and math. Once we had a rough draft of the completed manuscript, we shamelessly asked two outstanding colleagues to review the entire book. Both Philip Westbrook and Rob Knoeppel did not hesitate to support this project and both provided invaluable feedback that resulted in a better product. Finally, we wish to acknowledge the outstanding work of specific chief financial officers Tim Unrein and Bill Hungenberg, whose work and ideas related to budgeting resonate throughout this book.

Chapter 1

The Importance of Money in Public Education

In 1972 Liza Minelli and Joel Grey, in the movie *Cabaret*, popularized the familiar maxim "Money makes the world go round." This statement is particularly true in public education. The purpose of this book is to help aspiring P-12 budget managers appreciate the importance of money in the daily governance process of public education. Public funds are at the core of virtually every decision made in public education, and those leaders who develop the requisite skills to properly manage limited public funds are better positioned to maximize the potential of each dollar.

Over the past decade, we, the authors of this book, have taught school finance and budgeting to aspiring educational leaders at two different institutions, and our shared experience has helped us to recognize that many of the students who enroll in our courses do so with a degree of trepidation. Most aspiring educational leaders are not attracted to the position by the prospects of managing a school or department budget. However, the importance of proper management of public funds cannot be overstated.

It is our goal in our courses, and with this book, to not only stress the importance of school finance and budgeting for aspiring educational leaders, but also demonstrate the pleasure associated with properly managing money for the benefit of students. Indeed, we are convinced that the study of budgetary strategies is empowering and invigorating, and we hope to share this enthusiasm with each reader throughout this book. Ultimately, we will rate the success of our efforts with this book by the degree to which we are able to convince others of the joys found in properly managing budgets within public education.

The process of convincing the reader that managing a budget is exciting begins with a brief discussion of the importance of money in public education. Next, the discussion will shift to the importance of budgetary skills for

1

aspiring educational leaders. Finally, the chapter concludes with an overview of the organization of the book along with recommendations on how the reader should use it to increase his or her understanding of essential budgetary concepts and strategies.

THE IMPORTANCE OF MONEY

One cannot overstate the importance of resources in public education (as will be discussed later in the book, resources in public education include money, personnel, and time). Every decision made by educational leaders takes into consideration the potential fiscal impact of that decision on the school or school district. In a simple phrase, money truly matters. A lack of resources restricts the actions that educational leaders can take to better support students in the learning process. Conversely, an increase in resources affords educational leaders more options to better meet the needs of students.

For the 2011–2012 school year, the national average for per pupil spending was $10,667 (NCES, n.d.). Most advocates for public education, as well as public educators themselves, would contend that this per pupil funding level is insufficient to address all of the academic needs of students in the twenty-first century. However, the fiscal reality is that public education represents the greatest single line item for most state budgets, and it seems unlikely that there will be a drastic shift in the funding levels for public education in the near future. As a result, those entrusted with managing public school budgets must possess the skills to reduce inefficiency in spending practices and ensure that the limited budgets are used to maximize the educational benefit to all students.

The material contained in this book, along with the numerous activities geared to provide aspiring educational leaders with practical budget experience using real data, will help P-12 budget managers help develop the skills required to use current allocations effectively and efficiently. As a result, we would like to modify the statement made earlier. We do believe that money truly matters. However, we would like to alter this statement to read: Money truly matters and so does efficient management of existing funds.

THE IMPORTANCE OF BUDGET MANAGEMENT SKILLS

Educational leaders seek the opportunity to lead for a myriad of reasons. Most of these reasons are centered on students and recognize the importance of a strong leader's influence over the establishment and maintenance of a safe learning culture in the school or school district for all stakeholders (students, faculty, staff, parents, etc.). Few, if any, current educational leaders pursued formal leadership positions because they desired to manage, in some cases, multimillion-dollar budgets. And yet, ironically, in order for a leader to be effective in all other areas of the school governance process, this individual must be able to manage money.

One outstanding educational leader once stated, "The 'ances' will be the thing to get most people fired from administration—romance and finance." We do not want to see strong educational leaders lose their ability to positively impact a school climate due to preventable situations. We will leave the professional counseling related to romance in the workplace for others to explore; we will focus, instead, our ensuing discussion on the financial aspect of the job of leading a school or a school district.

Realizing that a majority educators entering leadership positions lack formal training related to managing a budget, the contents of this book will address the importance of budget management in detail. However, for this chapter, the focus on the importance of proper budget management will be limited to overarching concepts. These concepts will be presented as questions:

1. How much of a budget should be spent during the school year, and how much should be kept in reserve?
2. How do leaders decide which proposed expenditures to approve and which to reject?
3. What do leaders do if the organization's expenditures exceed the revenues?
4. How should leaders determine the benefit of current expenditures?
5. What potential inefficiencies in a school or school district can be eliminated without negatively impacting instructional practices?
6. Should budgets to departments, grade levels, or individual teachers be allocated using an incremental or zero-based budgeting approach?
7. Is performance pay an effective way to improve the overall quality of instruction?
8. What are the different restrictions placed on the various funding sources available to school leaders (title funds versus revenue from vending machines)?

These questions begin to illustrate the importance for educational leaders to possess budgeting knowledge, and even expertise, in public education. Our contention is that an educational leader who lacks a strong budgetary knowledge when assuming a leadership position will experience a steep learning curve to get "up to speed," and this lack of knowledge could result in significant job-related issues. We have crafted this book to provide aspiring educational leaders with both an overview of the theoretical concepts related to budgeting and the opportunity to put the theoretical concepts into practice through an array of budgetary exercises.

THE BOOK'S ORGANIZATION

This book is divided into four sections, which we are calling "phases" in the budgetary process. The focus of the first phase is on the foundational knowledge related to finance and budgeting that P-12 budget managers should possess. There are four chapters included in this phase. The first of these has a discussion on the basics of budget and finance (chapter 2), the second explores revenues and expenditures in public education (chapter 3), the third—an important chapter—explores financial ratio analysis (chapter 4), and the last discusses forecasting (chapter 5).

The main focus of the second phase is on the steps that P-12 budget managers must take to develop and oversee operating budgets for departments, schools, or school districts. This second phase contains two chapters. The budget cycle (chapter 6) is discussed in detail to ensure aspiring P-12 budget managers understand all of the steps involved in the process of developing and maintaining a budget. Next, the process related to overseeing, auditing, and analyzing the effectiveness of an existing budget (chapter 7) is explored.

In the third phase, we shift the discussion to capital budgeting. This phase is divided into two chapters. In chapter 8, the discussion centers on funding capital projects without accruing debt (in the form of a bond). Next, we explore the concepts related to funding capital projects while accruing debt (chapter 9). The focus of the fourth phase is simply alignment. Ultimately, a P-12 budget manager should ensure that spending practices align with the organization's vision statement, mission statement, goals, and strategic plan (chapter 10).

PARTING THOUGHTS BEFORE THE FUN BEGINS

An interesting exercise is to ask standing P-12 administrators which aspect of their jobs they felt the least prepared to take on when they graduated with their principal license or when they started off as a principal. For a vast majority of current leaders the answer will be related to budgeting. In addition, most aspiring educational leaders, when they start their graduate studies to earn a principal license, lack a working understanding of P-12 budgets. Unfortunately, most principal preparation programs dedicate only a limited amount of time to exploring the budgetary strategies, and the assumption is that principals will be taught, while on the job, how to properly oversee a budget.

We, obviously, feel this lack of attention to properly prepare aspiring educational leaders to create, manage, and oversee a P-12 budget is dangerous and shortsighted. As a result, we wrote this book to support aspiring educational leaders and to provide those invested in preparing quality educational leaders for the twenty-first century with a tool that will bolster understanding of core budgetary theories and practices.

Our vision is that this book will aid in the development of complete educational leaders by instilling in aspiring principals a working understanding of P-12 budgets and of how to maximize the spending power of each dollar. For example, consider this question: What percent of inefficiency, or money poorly spent, is permissible in a public school budget? Ideally, the answer would be "zero percent," but we are not sure that is realistic. So, the answer must be "as little as possible." We are certain that the concepts covered in this book will empower aspiring educational leaders to identify and work to eliminate inefficiencies in P-12 budgets.

Finally, an educational leader with a strong conceptual and practical understanding of how to create, manage, and oversee a P-12 budget will quickly discover the joy associated with this vital knowledge. This leader will be able to say "Yes" to teachers with innovative proposed expenditures for improving the educational experiences of students due to the high efficiency of the budget as opposed to the leader who has to always say, "That is a great idea, but there isn't any money to make it happen."

GUIDING QUESTIONS

The following questions address many of the key concepts covered in this chapter. Ideally, the reader should be able to answer each of these questions upon completion of the reading. If that is not the case, then we recommend that the reader review the different concepts to solidify his or her understanding of the topics.

1. What is the importance of money in public education?
2. What are the three types of resources in public education? How will you, as an aspiring educational leader, manage each of these resources?
3. What are examples of inefficiency in public education? (Note, this was not specifically covered in the chapter, but we think the reader should begin to identify examples of inefficiencies in public education.)
4. Why is it essential for educational leaders to develop and refine their budget management skills?
5. Why is managing a budget a joy?

ADDITIONAL READING

For the readers that would like additional information on the topics addressed in chapter 1, we offer the following recommendations:

Brimley, Jr., V., D. A. Verstegen, & R. R. Garfield. 2012. *Financing education in a climate of change*. Boston, MA: Pearson. (In particular, pay attention to chapter 1.)

Cox, B., S. C. Weiler, & L. M. Cornelius. 2013. *The costs of education: Revenues and spending in public, private and charter schools*. Lancaster, PA: ProActive. (In particular, pay attention to chapter 1.)

Thompson, D. C., R. C. Wood, & F. E. Crampton. 2008. *Money and schools* (4th ed.). Larchmont, NY: Eye on Education. (In particular, pay attention to chapter 1.)

EXERCISES

The exercises related to chapter 1 are aimed at providing the reader with context for better understanding all of the financial and budgetary concepts that will be explored throughout this book. As a result, students are encouraged to do the following:

1. Access a school district's budget report. The school district will, preferably, be the one where the reader works, where applicable. Once accessed, read the executive summary closely. Then, peruse the rest of the document. You will be asked to refer back to this document throughout the book, so retain an accessible copy of the budget.
2. State departments of education publish an annual update to help laypeople understand school finance. Readers are to search for and access this document and then read it. For example, in Colorado the document is called *Understanding Colorado School Finance and Categorical Program Funding*, and the 2013 edition is available at: http://www.cde.state.co.us/sites/default/files/FY2013-14%20Brochure.pdf.

Phase I

FOUNDATION

The first phase of this book will focus on the foundational knowledge an aspiring P-12 budget manager and educational leader must possess in order to effectively oversee public funds. Specifically, the reader will first explore revenues, where these dollars come from, and how funds are distributed from the state to the school district to the local school. In addition, the reader will learn about expenditures and what happens if expenditures exceed anticipated revenues.

Finally, the foundational knowledge that aspiring P-12 budget managers should possess includes the use of financial ratios and forecasting. These concepts will provide P-12 budget managers with the skills necessary to manage a budget in a way that provides all students with an adequate educational opportunity.

Chapter 2

Getting to Know a Budget

Yukl (2002, p. 2) observed that "most definitions of leadership reflect the assumption that it involves a process whereby intentional influence is exerted by one person over other people to guide, structure, and facilitate activities and relationships in a group or an organization." Leadership skills are essential for an educational organization to improve, and the dearth of leadership can negatively impact an organization for years. However, aspiring P-12 educational leaders rarely begin the journey of formal leadership training with a strong understanding of public budgeting. Instead, they demonstrate prowess in other areas essential to leadership—interpersonal skills, motivation, vision, curriculum, and so on—and the assumption is that the less innate skills, such a properly overseeing a budget, can be learned.

The irony in the current development of educational organization leadership is that aspiring leaders are typically required to complete one course in the area of finance and budgeting. Inevitably, graduates of P-12 educational leadership programs are hired for positions when they lack all of the required skills to properly oversee large budgets in a way that allows public dollars to drive the organization toward improvement.

The purpose of this book is to supplement the theoretical training related to finance and budgeting and provide both aspiring and standing educational leaders with the opportunity to develop a working understanding of the budgetary process. Readers will be asked to "crunch numbers" throughout this book in an effort to transform theoretical concepts into real activities and, ultimately, to increase understanding.

The process of demystifying budgets for educational organizations begins with steps that can be taken to better understand a budget. This chapter is

9

divided into four sections. First, an explanation as to why a budget is essential to educational organizations is presented. Second, a discussion on different managerial approaches to allocating funds that educational leaders can utilize is presented. Third, the revenue sources and expenditure allocations are presented. Finally, the importance of educational leaders developing a philosophy related to managing budgets is explained.

WHY BUDGETS?

One of the mysteries of life is that, regardless of a person's personal income, *wants* almost always surpass revenues. We never seem to make enough money to do all that we want to do. Against this backdrop, the answer to the question "Why do I need to know about budgets?" should be clear. P-12 educational leaders lack sufficient resources to do all they would like to do, and a budget plays an essential role in ensuring that all of their *needs* are funded. In addition, a well-crafted budget allows educational leaders to prioritize *wants* so that the most pressing items are funded as well.

What are the needs in education? In P-12 education, the greatest budgetary *need* relates to personnel. Personnel costs typically account for roughly 80% of the total general operating fund or annual budget (Cox, Weiler, & Cornelius, 2013, pp. 62–63). *Needs* would also include costs associated with operations and maintenance of facilities, transportation, police services, and debt service. On the other hand, *wants* are specific to each educational organization. For example, a public high school might *want* a swimming pool, or an elementary school might *want* to hire a literacy interventionist. In general, a budget enables educational leaders to maximize the potential of the limited resources they oversee. What follows is a discussion on the purpose of a P-12 education budget.

P-12 BUDGET: THE PURPOSE

A P-12 budget is typically compared to an equilateral triangle, with revenues, expenditures, and programs making up the three sides (Odden & Picus, 2008, p. 236). This is depicted in Figure 2.1.

The interplay of revenues, expenditures, and programs exemplified in Figure 2.1 serves to identify the purpose of a P-12 budget. School districts operate with limited funds, and school officials must balance programs and expenditures with revenues in an effective manner to ensure the vision, mission, and goals of the district are being met. Each of the three items is discussed below.

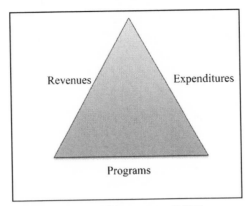

Figure 2.1   Budget Triangle. *Source*: Odden & Picus (2008).

Revenue

Public education is funded with tax dollars, and these monies come from a combination of federal, state, and local revenue sources. Revenues can also be supplemented with a voter-approved mill levy override, where voters in the school district agree to provide the school district with additional funds for specific educational purposes. Ultimately, the state determines the amount of revenues available to local school districts. Revenue sources are discussed in greater detail later in this chapter.

Expenditure

One of the biggest challenges facing P-12 educational leaders is to accurately anticipate expenditures for each fiscal year. The process of anticipating expenditures begins with a detailed analysis of personnel costs—including benefits for teachers, administrators, and all other staff members—since this single item typically accounts for over 80% of the total program.

Other expenditures are more difficult to anticipate. Is the copier machine going to break? Will the middle school need a new roof? Are gas prices going to remain relatively stable? The challenge for P-12 educational leaders is to spend virtually all of the funds in the total program, or annual budget, in a fiscally responsible manner each year. To have excess in reserve at the end of the school year is to deny students in the system all the educational benefit they are entitled to and to exceed the total program is not an option.

Program

The final piece to the P-12 school district budget is the maintenance of programs that are benefiting students. Fiscally responsible educational leaders should regularly analyze program expenditures to determine if the current effort is both effective and cost-effective. For example, if a reading program is generating a certain amount of growth, could another, less expensive, program produce the same (if not better) results?

The purpose of the P-12 budget is to ensure that the available funds are spent in a way that aligns with the school district's vision, mission statement, and goals. These funds should benefit students, and the budget is a tool that educational leaders can use to ensure that public funds are being spent judiciously.

ALLOCATING BUDGET FUNDS

Once the P-12 organization (be it a school or a school district) receives funds, the leader, working collaboratively with a governing body, must take steps to allocate these funds into various budgetary categories. There are a number of ways in which leaders can approach the allocation of budgetary funds, and the four most salient approaches are discussed below. Four specific P-12 approaches to allocating funds are discussed in detail below.

When allocating funds to different budgetary categories, there are two overarching principles that leaders should be mindful of: efficiency and effectiveness. The main idea behind efficiency is to ensure that the allocation process is not placing too much of an unreasonable burden on teachers. If the allocation process is inefficient, then people might opt to go without the funds. If that is the case, students will, at the very least, miss out on learning opportunities.

In addition, an allocation process must be effective. The money has to get to where it is needed most in a timely manner. How is this done? The four different allocation approaches discussed below enable P-12 leaders to disseminate funds to various organizations and individuals.

Student-Based Budgeting

Student-based budgeting, also referred to as school-based budgeting, provides the principal of a building with all of the funds deemed necessary by school district officials to run the school for a fiscal year. This includes, most importantly, the personnel costs. Under a student-based budget, a building principal receives a budget that includes millions of dollars (depending upon the size of the school) for personnel salaries and benefits. Under a more traditional (and nonstudent-based) allocation process, personnel allocations are controlled at the district level, and school principals are told how many teachers will staff their buildings each year.

Advantage

The biggest advantage to this approach of allocating resources is that building principals, who know the specific needs of schools, are empowered to allocate limited resources to better meet the needs of all students. In addition, building-level personnel must become better stewards of limited public funds, thus increasing efficiency.

Disadvantage

The most glaring disadvantage to student-based budgeting is that most principals are not properly trained to oversee multimillion-dollar budgets. As a result, there is a greater potential for financial impropriety. In addition, building-level principals are hired to be educational leaders for schools. The added responsibilities of overseeing large budgets can result in less time being dedicated to ensuring all students receive meaningful instruction.

Zero-Based Budgeting

Zero-based budgeting operates under the assumption that each budgetary category or account (at the school level, examples would include a teacher's supplies account, a department's budget, etc.) receives no money at the beginning of the fiscal year. Then, departments, grade levels, and individuals are invited to submit expenditure proposals that will, ideally, be reviewed by a building leadership team (this team should consist of the principal and other personnel in leadership capacities).

This approach increases the transparency of the process and is essential for zero-based budgeting to effectively impact the allocation of resources since the decision-making process becomes collaborative. Those expenditure proposals that are deemed in alignment with the school's vision, mission, and goals are approved, whereas those expenditure proposals that do not align with the direction of the school are denied.

Advantage

This allocation approach ensures there is no frantic rush to spend funds ineffectively at the end of the school year to make sure those funds are not lost in future fiscal cycles. In addition, zero-based budgeting guarantees that approved expenditures are aligned with the focus of the school.

Disadvantage

A disadvantage to zero-based budgeting is that it is time consuming. Some teachers may shy away from having to justify proposed expenditures and, as a result, may not even submit a proposal for review. In addition, denying proposed expenditures may create a culture of favoritism and mistrust within the building (however, this final disadvantage can be significantly mitigated, if not completely eliminated, by a fully transparent decision-making process).

Incremental Budgeting

Incremental budgeting takes the amount of money that was allocated to each subcategory in a budget during the previous fiscal year and reallocates that amount, with slight alterations to control for changes to the current fiscal year budget allocation, to the next fiscal year budget. For example, if the social studies department of a high school received $1,500 for the previous fiscal year allocation and the school's overall budget did not change at all for the next fiscal year cycle, then, under an incremental budgeting process, the social studies department would receive the same amount, $1,500, for the next fiscal year as well.

Advantage

Incremental budgeting is the least time consuming of all of the approaches discussed in this section. Moreover, it does not require that expenditure proposals be reviewed.

Disadvantage

The most significant examples of misallocation of limited resources in public education typically occur under an incremental approach to allocating resources. Incremental budgeting diminishes the amount of supervision over proposed expenditures; however, there is still a degree of accountability. Finally, incremental budgeting encourages poor spending decisions when it is coupled with a "spend it or lose it" policy since people would rather make questionable spending decisions to ensure a similar budget in the future.

Budget Hybrids in P-12

Which allocation approach is optimal for public P-12 education? The answer to that essential question is that "it depends." There are situations where a student-based budget approach might make the most sense, and there are others where an incremental approach is optimal. The effective leader will tap into the advantages of each of the approaches to allocating resources to maximize the impact of each dollar. For example, if all teachers in a building are going to require copy paper, then an incremental approach to funds for copy paper would be most effective and efficient.

If, on the other hand, the science department needed a significant amount of money to upgrade the science lab, then a zero-based approach would make the most sense (and, in this scenario, the English department may receive only a paltry budget allocation). Regardless of the approach, transparency in the decision-making process is essential. The P-12 leader must include others in the school in the decision-making process and be willing to explain how decisions were made.

MAJOR BUDGETING CATEGORIES

In nearly every facet of education budgeting and planning, a central concern for those charged with administering resources is the appropriate use of revenues and the efficient management and containment of expenditures. In order to effectively support strategic and core priorities, budget managers in education should become acquainted with the typical sources of revenues and expenditures that will help their school or school district achieve its varied goals and objectives. The major resource and allocation categories faced by budget managers are presented in this section.

P-12 Budgeting: Revenue

Public education is funded with public funds. Typically, these public dollars are generated through a combination of multiple sources: federal, state, and local dollars. The revenue sources for P-12 budgeting are summarized in Table 2.1.

The average revenue sources reported in Table 2.1 are from a national perspective. The specific revenue sources will vary from state to state. For those states that do not have one of the taxes listed in Table 2.1, the total revenue for public education is generated differently. In states that do not have an income tax, such as Florida and Nevada, revenues generated from the tourism industry are used to supplant the lost revenue from not levying a tax on income. Other states that lack a robust tourism industry may rely only on some of the taxes identified in Table 2.1 to generate the total dollars for

Table 2.1   Revenue Sources for P-12 Budgeting

Level	Tax(es)	Percent of Total Budget for Public Education	Total Dollars
Federal	Income	9.6	56,730,664,000
State	Income Sales Lottery	46.7	277,079,518,000
Local	Property Ownership	43.7	259,250,999,000
Total		100	593,061,181,000

Note: The actual dollars reported are for the 2008–2009 school year (NCES, 2011).

public education. In such cases, the state will generate more revenue from the remaining taxes. For example, if a state does not levy a tax on property, then it stands to reason that the state's income or sales tax rates or both are higher—this would be its way of compensating for the revenue lost as a result of not taxing properties.

Revenues in P-12 education are primarily based upon the number of students enrolled in each school district. Each state has a funding formula that, in the end, provides each school district with a specific dollar amount for each student enrolled. The specific dollar amount, or the per pupil expenditure, is generated from a combination of federal, state, and local tax dollars.

Some school districts are able to access additional revenues in the form of a voter-approved mill levy override. Essentially, a mill levy override is authorization from the voters to provide the local school district with additional funds annually (and in most cases indefinitely) generated from an increased tax on property. There is a multitude of variations on mill levy overrides. For example, some voters will only approve a mill levy override with a sunset, or a termination date for the additional funds. Others will approve mill levy overrides with vague wording in the ballot measure, whereas some others will demand specific explanations about how the funds are to be spent. From a school district's perspective, school district officials will enjoy a greater degree of flexibility when it comes to spending voter-approved mill levy funds the more vague the wording of the approved override.

However, in order to successfully pass a proposed mill levy override, it is essential that school district officials take the necessary steps to understand how local voters feel about school district–related issues. Specifically, school district officials can administer attitude surveys throughout the community, or they can employ an outside agency to collect these data independently. Surveys can be conducted either over the phone or by mail. The phone approach is more expensive but produces a greater response rate.

In addition, school district officials need to be involved in various organizations throughout the community. This step allows for the leaders to interact with community members, specifically reference the good that is occurring in the school district, and, ultimately, obtain a sense of the concerns that community members have related to the direction of the school district. This type of information will provide school district officials with a better sense of how the community would vote on a proposed mill levy override and with essential information on how best to craft the proposed ballot measure.

P-12 Budgeting: Allocation

An interesting fact when considering a P-12 school district (or school) budget is the lack of discretionary funds. A vast majority of the allocations in a P-12

Table 2.2 P-12 Budget Allocations, Nationally

Allocation Category	Allocation Percent of Total Budget
Instruction—teachers	62.9
Support services—counselors, paraprofessionals, administrative assistants	7.5
Administration	7.6
Operations and maintenance	10.0
Transportation	4.5
Food services and other	7.5
Total	100

Source: NCES, 2010.

budget are directed to fixed costs. Assuming those fixed costs are appropriately allocated and managed, it stands to reason that there is not a lot of room for inefficiencies in public education as a result of the fixed costs. The national averages of P-12 budget allocations are reported in Table 2.2.

An analysis of Table 2.2 results in a few conclusions. First, public education is an industry dependent upon people. According to the data reported in the table, 78% of all funds for public education are dedicated to salaries and benefits for personnel (the first three allocation categories reported in Table 2.2 represent personnel expenses). In some school districts that percentage rises above 80%.

A second conclusion from Table 2.2 focuses on inefficiencies. If all of the personnel allocations are appropriate, which is not always a safe assumption, then 78% of the allocation is efficient. A majority of the remaining allocation categories—operations and maintenance, transportation, and food services—represent fixed costs that must be incorporated into the total program or annual budget. Once all of these fixed costs are combined with the personnel allocations, school districts are left with roughly 3% in the other category. As a result, an argument could be made that school districts are operating at a 97% efficiency rate, if the personnel and fixed costs are void of inefficiencies.

This observation on efficiency is not to imply that school district officials should assume funds are being allocated and spent in an efficient manner. Rather, the point is to stress that there is not a discretionary allocation in public education. Given this fact, along with the fact that public educators are stewards of public funds, school district officials must vigilantly look to identifying and eradicating waste and inefficiency.

Operating and Capital Budgets: Basic Difference

The basic distinction between operating and capital budgets centers on the focus of each budget. Operating budgets are those budgets that comprise the financial operations for the day-to-day running of the institution during a fiscal year, including revenues, reserves, and current expenditures. Conversely, capital budgets provide funding for new construction or significant facility renovations that take on a longer useful life (Goldstein, 2012).

Capital budgets play a significant role in covering long-term (more than one year) and major P-12 expenditures, usually by issuing debt in the form of bonds. The difficulty for school district officials is recognizing and understanding when, where, and how they can or should access this funding mechanism given the large amount of deferred maintenance many institutions face, especially in the public-sector.

It is important for budget managers to recognize that bonding is not the optimal way to fund capital projects, especially repair projects, since it constitutes funding construction projects with debt. This is of vital importance given the fact that debt service (payments due on debt incurred) and depreciation costs become part of the operating budget, and thus operating expenses.

PHILOSOPHY OF BUDGET MANAGEMENT

In previous sections we have covered a number of comprehensive approaches to budgeting and budgeting categories. In this final section the discussion turns to the philosophy underpinning the manner in which new budget managers might approach the task of actually administering the budget. Because schools and school districts often have a long history of doing things in a particular way—institutional traditions—understanding, integrating, and possibly overcoming these practices and inertia are of significance for those becoming familiar with the budgeting process of a particular institution.

As a new budget manager, a good place to start obtaining information may be determining which budgeting approach the school or school district already employs. For example, certain budget approaches suggest a more centralized approach, such as incremental budgeting. On the other hand, approaches like student-based budgeting provide a much more decentralized approach to budget management. Regardless of the type of approach used within the school district, some new budget managers might find that they are inclined to more or less centralized budget administration.

As with any management approach, there are positives and negatives associated with each course of action. Again, it is necessary to reiterate the notion that like budget approaches in general, a single, comprehensive method for overseeing budgets is unlikely. Most managers will develop a hybrid style that best reflects their philosophy of budget management and balance it with institutional or school needs and mission. As stated earlier, a hybrid approach to allocating revenues allows a leader to utilize the advantages of different approaches in an optimal manner. Educational leaders must never become too committed to one approach to allocating resources. Instead, situational factors should contribute to the determination of the optimal allocation strategy

Apart from the philosophical perspective taken by the budget manager, there are a few things everyone should consider. First, the new budget manager should carefully examine the character of the school district. For example, what are the goals, mission, short- and long-term objectives of the school district, and how does the budget align with these stated priorities? Additionally, what are the formal and informal mechanisms that undergird the resource allocation process and decision-making, and how does my management style fit into this process?

Second, a new budget manager should determine the degree of transparency within the budgetary process. An important question that must be asked is whether the institution's character supports broad inclusion of individuals, units, programs, offices, and so on in the deliberation over resource allocation? Closely related to this question is whether there exists a significant level of trust among stakeholders. If the budget process is opaque and trust is minimal, it is likely that an unhealthy climate will develop and manifest itself in the budget process and final document (the best illustration of this point can be seen in certain school districts where, due to a long-standing history of mistrust, contract negotiations between school district officials and the local teachers' association become difficult). Again, the philosophical perspective taken by the budget manager can contribute positively or negatively to this process.

Third, and finally, communication with budget units, other financial officers, and stakeholders around campus, at the main office, or at other schools should be of paramount importance. By communicating effectively and often throughout the budget process, the likelihood of distrust developing is diminished.

The goal of the budget manager should be to help budgeting move along smoothly while keeping the community appraised of changes and to avoid surprises whenever possible (Goldstein, 2012). This course of action will help avert situations where distrust, gossip, rumors, or counterproductive behaviors arise. The philosophical perspective taken by the budget manager should seek to encourage a culture of communication. In other words, share information and communicate, communicate, communicate!

CONCLUSION

The purpose of this chapter was to provide the reader with a theoretical overview of a budget in P-12 education. This theoretical foundation related to a budget is essential as readers engage in the different activities incorporated in this book. All of the activities are aimed at taking theoretical components of working with budgets in an education setting and providing practical application. Ultimately, students of school and school district budgets are encouraged to develop and refine their own budgetary philosophy.

GUIDING QUESTIONS

The following questions address many of the key concepts addressed in chapter 2. The reader should be able to answer each of these questions once finished with the reading. If that is not the case, then we recommend that the reader review the different sections to solidify understanding of the concepts.

1. Why do we budget? What's the point?
2. What is the purpose of budgeting? How are budgeting decisions made in your unit, office, program, institution, and/or department? How does this relate to day-to-day activities?
3. Which budget approach do you think is the most useful? Why? Why are hybrid budget approaches becoming more popular? Do you know the approach that will be or is currently being used to make budgeting decisions?
4. What are the fundamental differences between operating and capital budgets? Why are they different?
5. Thinking broadly, how does the budget philosophy of decision-makers matter in the budgeting process and for the fiscal administration as a whole?

ADDITIONAL READING

Those readers desiring additional information on the concepts addressed in chapter 2 should consult the following:

Odden, A., & S. Archibald,. 2001. *Reallocating resources: How to boost student achievement without asking for more.* Thousand Oaks, CA: Corwin Press.
Odden, A. R., & L. O. Picus. 2014. *School finance: A policy perspective* (5th ed.). New York, NY: McGraw Hill. (Please refer specifically to chapter 12.)
Sorenson, R. D., & L. M. Goldsmith. 2013. *The principal's guide to school budgeting* (2nd ed.). Thousand Oaks, CA: Corwin Press. (Please refer specifically to chapter 5.)

EXERCISES

The exercises related to chapter 2 are designed to enhance the work done in chapter 1 and to give the reader additional context for understanding the finance and budget concepts embedded throughout this book. Students are encouraged to do the following:

1. Interview at least one school-level administrative assistant over bookkeeping, at least one building principal, and, where possible, the chief financial officer for the school district. Note, these interviews could be conducted via email if that proves more convenient for the participants. Ask each person you interview the following questions:
   a. Why are budgets important in public education?
   b. What do I need to know about budgets as an aspiring educational leader?
   c. What are the advantages and disadvantages with incremental budgeting, zero-based budgeting, and student-based budgeting?
   d. What percent of the school district's budget goes to personnel costs (including benefits)?
   e. What are important points to consider as I work on developing my own philosophy related to managing budgets?
2. Using the school district budget that you accessed for chapter 1, determine the actual allocations of revenue sources (compare to the national averages reported in Table 2.1) and the actual budget allocations for this school district (compare to the national averages reported in Table 2.2).
3. Rate the taxes levied to fund public education (see Table 2.1) based on the following criteria:
   a. Equity—how fair is the tax?
   b. Impact—how big of an impact is the tax on individuals?
   c. Administration—how much of the revenue goes to administer the tax?
   d. Yield—how much revenue does the tax generate?

Chapter 3

Anticipating Revenues
and Expenditures

In educational contexts, for those charged with overseeing budgets on a day-to-day basis, understanding the basics of revenue structure and generation is of central concern. Budget managers and planners at schools and school districts must recognize the value of both anticipating revenues and revenue volatility.

The other side of the budgeting process is concerned with anticipating and understanding expenditures in public education. The public nature of education means that, for the most part, P-12 educational budget managers are working under a great deal of uncertainty. The study of anticipating expenditures and understanding fluctuations is essential to effectively overseeing and managing P-12 budgets. The purpose of this chapter is to provide the reader with a working understanding of P-12 revenues and expenditures.

WHAT ARE REVENUES?

For the most part, total revenue is best understood as a relationship between *price* and *quantity*, if employing typical finance and economic theory as a guide (Parkin, 2010). For example, in private firms that produce a measureable quantity of products or services, one simply needs to multiply the number of the good or service sold by its price to obtain the total revenues. This basic relationship is presented by the following equation:

$$\text{Price} \times \text{Quantity} = \text{Total Revenue}.$$

This equation makes perfect sense for estimating total revenues derived from countable quantities with easily measured benefits. However, the public nature of education can render this equation inappropriate for measuring total revenues. This is because the price of the "product" in education is not easily measured. Additionally, the quantity of the "product" in education is also difficult to estimate.[1] We delve into the particulars of these concerns in the next section on revenues for public education.

REVENUES FOR P-12

The discussion of revenues for P-12 public education must consider both macro- and micro-perspectives. From the macro-perspective of revenues for P-12 public education, students, practitioners, and scholars of public education finance and budgeting must know the origins of public revenues. The micro-perspective focuses on revenues from a school district's chief financial officer's point of view. Each of these perspectives is discussed in detail in this section. However, prior to this detailed discussion, educational leaders need to recognize the different types of resources that must be managed efficiently. Resources in public education include:

1. Money—the obvious resource that administrators oversee is the public money allocated to schools and school districts for the education of children. The effective and efficient management of revenues in public education is the primary focus of this book.
2. Time—a second finite resource is time. Educators have a set amount of time to support children in the learning process. For this reason, administrators must take the necessary steps to ensure that all within the school or school district are maximizing the potential of each minute through meaningful instruction.
3. Personnel—the final finite resource that administrators must manage properly is the allocation of personnel for instruction and support services.

The Origins of P-12 Revenues

Public education is funded almost exclusively from public tax revenues. These tax revenues are generated at all three levels of government—local, state, and federal. The taxes typically levied at these levels are summarized in Table 3.1

It should be noted that the data presented in Table 3.1 are typical and not necessarily reflective of all 50 states. For example, certain states do not levy an income tax or a sales tax. In states where certain taxes do not exist, other taxes or revenue sources, such as tourism or natural resources, are required to generate a greater percentage of the funding for P-12 public education.

Table 3.1 Taxes Levied at All Levels of Government

Level of Government	Type of Tax(es)	Percent of the Total Allocation for P-12
Federal	Income tax	5–7
State	Income tax Sales tax Lottery tax	45–50
Local	Property tax Ownership tax	45–50

Each tax listed in Table 3.1 has its particular strengths and weaknesses. To better understand the strengths and weaknesses of each tax requires a brief discussion on the characteristics of an ideal tax system. Odden and Picus (2014, p. 349) offered the following criteria to evaluate the effectiveness of a tax:

- Yield—the amount of revenues the tax produces.
- Equity—the fairness of the tax.
- The Elasticity of the Tax—examines how the tax responds to economic upswings and downturns. Ideally, a tax is extremely responsive during upswings (generating more revenues when a state or the federal economy is growing) and unresponsive during downturns (revenues do not go down during a recession).
- Administration—the amount of money required to administer the tax. The higher the cost of administration, the lower the revenues available for public programs such as P-12 education.

An examination of the taxes listed in Table 3.1 using the evaluation criteria from Odden and Picus illustrates the strengths and weaknesses of each tax. Since income, sales, lottery, and property taxes account for a majority of the funding for P-12 public education, each is analyzed in Table 3.2 using the aforementioned criteria.

One point illustrated in Table 3.2 is the fact that there is not one perfect tax. In fact, the practice of most states is to use a combination of most, if not all, of these taxes to fund public education.[2] The combination of these taxes creates a system of taxation that is preferable to the alternative of relying exclusively on any one of the taxes identified in the table.

Brimley, Verstegen, and Garfield (2012, p. 113) presented the following equation to model how taxes produce revenues for P-12 public education:

$$\text{Tax Base} \times \text{Tax Rate} = \text{Tax Yield}.$$

The tax yield, or revenue, is derived from the tax base multiplied by the tax rate. Tax base refers to the group of taxpayers to which the tax rate is applied.

Table 3.2   Rating Taxes Used to Fund Public Education

Criterion	Income Tax	Sales Tax	Property Tax and Ownership Tax	Lottery Tax
Yield	High	High	High	Low
Equity	High	Low	Low	Low
Elasticity	Low	Moderate	High	High
Administration	Expensive	Inexpensive	Moderately expensive	Extremely expensive

For example, property owners pay, either directly or indirectly (through the rent charged to tenets), property tax and gamblers pay the lottery tax.

P-12 Revenues from a School District's Perspective

Revenues for a school district or school do not typically take into consideration the yield or the elasticity of a tax. Instead, the revenues for a school district originate from the state's general assembly and are based on the number of students the school district is educating. The formula used to model revenues for school districts is represented below:

$$\text{Per Pupil Operating Revenue}^3 \times \text{Student Population} = \text{School District Total Program.}$$

Per pupil operating revenue (PPOR) refers to the amount of money the school district receives from the state for each child it educates. The PPOR figure is multiplied by the number of students enrolled in each school district. This gives the school district's total program, or its annual budget. The PPOR figure fluctuates from year to year, as exemplified by the data presented in Table 3.3, which illustrates the variance in funding between states.

Voter-Approved Mill Levy Override

There is an additional revenue source that is available to all school districts, contingent upon voter approval. School district officials can approach voters living within the boundaries of the school district to obtain permission to levy additional mills on property owners in the form of a mill levy override. These monies are added to the total program of the school district. For example, if a school district's total program was $120,000,000, and voters had approved a $10,000,000 mill levy override, then the actual budget for the school district would be $130,000,000.

There are a number of different approaches to mill levy overrides, and the most typical ones are briefly discussed below:

Table 3.3 Per Pupil Operating Revenue (PPOR), 2009–2010 to 2013–2014

School Year	Highest PPOR ($)	Lowest PPOR ($)	US Average ($)
2008–2009	Wyoming (19,389)	Nevada (7,630)	11,521
2009–2010	Wyoming (19,576)	Nevada (7,599)	11,841
2010–2011	Vermont (20,572)	Nevada (7,582)	12,037
2011–2012	Vermont (21,924)	Nevada (7,473)	11,994
2012–2013	Vermont (23,485)	Nevada (7,507)	12,231

1. Mill Amount: Some mill levy overrides ask voters to approve adding a set number of mills to the school district's total program. Realizing that the value of a mill is based off of the net assessed value of all the properties within the school district's boundaries and that the value of properties, in general, increases with time, the advantage of this approach is that the total value of the mill levy override will increase with time (assuming the value of property increases).

2. Dollar Amount: Some school districts will approach voters with a proposed mill levy override that has a specific dollar amount. The major problem with this approach is that the actual value of the approved dollar amount will decrease with time due to inflation. As a result, the specific dollar amount will lose buying power with time.

3. Mill Levy Override with a Sunset: Unless otherwise specified, a voter-approved mill levy override will generate the approved amount of funding for the school district indefinitely. However, some voters are hesitant to approve a mill levy override without a degree of accountability. In these more fiscally conservative communities, school district officials will place a sunset on the mill levy override. As a result, school district officials in these more conservative communities ask voters to approve a mill levy override for a set duration, for example, five years, and then as the override is about to expire the officials go back to the voters and ask for a new mill levy override.

A final thought related to mill levy overrides. In the ballot initiative that voters are asked to approve, school district officials will use either specific or general terminology on how the money will be spent. The specific language is, ultimately, determined by the preliminary survey work to determine voter trends. However, more specific language in the mill levy override will result in less spending options in the future. For example, if a mill levy override states that the money will be used to purchase interactive whiteboards and projectors, then the school district is required to spend the money accordingly. A more general term that would be less restrictive for future school district officials would be that the money will be spent on technology to enhance classroom instruction.

The biggest challenge for budget managers in P-12 public education is to accurately forecast student enrollments each year. Forecasting strategies will be briefly touched on in this chapter and explained in greater detail in chapter 5. The nuances of this challenge cannot be minimized. For example, how is a budget manager supposed to know how many students will enroll in kindergarten each year? Or how do school district officials control for student mobility, those who move in and out of the school district, each year?

The answers to such questions are at the heart of the role of the budget manager in accurately forecasting budgets for the upcoming school year. In addition, a budget manager is well served to keep abreast of legislative trends within the state that could positively or negatively impact a school district's budget. Included in this chapter are exercises that will help aspiring budget managers begin to develop and refine the necessary skillset to accurately forecast a school district budget for an upcoming school year.

ACCURATELY FORECASTING AND FORECASTING ACCURACY

As external and internal forces can impact the revenue generating capacity of schools and school districts, it is important for forecasters to carry out "what if" analyses (Rylee, 2011). In this instance, the goal is to stress the importance of accurately forecasting revenues based on available data and information. An additional goal is the consideration of multiple scenarios where worst- and best-case scenarios are considered. For example, extensive economic turbulence or changes in the political landscape can materially impact P-12 education budgets. Moreover, by accounting for possible fluctuations, including valid and appropriate data, and providing reasonable, if not conservative, revenue estimates, the budget planner can provide forecasts with a great deal of accuracy. This is not to suggest, however, that forecasts will be exact.

It is not unusual for forecasts to be off by a relatively small amount. However, in some instances, even the best forecasting techniques, information, and data will fall short of the mark. This is because forecasting is an estimate of future trends based on available data, which might not be complete. Certain undetermined events cannot always be accurately predicted.

A good case in point is the crash of the housing market in 2008, which initially impacted property values and local tax receipts. The 2008 recession provides a good sense of what forecasters face related to uncertainty. Still, high-quality revenue forecasting can provide a great deal of decision-making information and can also help education budgeters anticipate fluctuations in their revenue streams. While some limitations exist, the usefulness of forecasting remains evident as budget concerns continue to be a central focus.

The key to this entire discussion is for aspiring P-12 budget managers to appreciate the importance of fiscal conservatism when it comes to managing public funds. Fiscal conservatism simply refers to managing funds in a manner that retains resources in reserve in case of an emergency. The concept of fiscal conservatism can be illustrated by the following equation:

Underestimating Revenues + Overestimating Expenditures
= Fiscal Conservatism.

P-12 budget managers that practice fiscal conservatism are, typically, able to more efficiently and effectively manage public resources with a long-term plan in mind. Such budget managers are proactive as opposed to reactive.

EXPENDITURES AND COSTS

As noted by Finkler et al. (2013), defining and measuring costs and expenditures are highly complex processes. The reason for this complexity is related to the varied costs categories that exist. Here we present a number of costs that are typically included in the analysis of cost structures; however, please note that this list is not exhaustive.

Definitions of Typical Costs in Education

Finkler et al. (2013) and Goldstein (2012) offered the following definitions for the typical costs that P-12 budget managers will encounter:

1. Direct Cost—Costs that are traceable back to the direct production of a good or service, or project or activity. In education, instruction is often treated as a direct cost.
2. Indirect Cost—Costs that are not readily traceable back to a project or activity, or to the production of a good or service. In education, a typical example of an indirect cost is the maintenance or depreciation of a building.
3. Variable Cost—Costs that vary with the level of production of a good or service, or with volume changes in an activity or program. An example would again be instruction given that costs change directly as more instructors are hired or let go.
4. Fixed Cost—Costs that do not vary with changes in the level of production of a good or service, or with volume changes in an activity or program. Again, physical plant would be a good example since the cost of the building is fixed, though maintenance might fall under variable costs.

5. Semi-Variable Cost—Costs that vary partially related to the productions of goods or services, or to changes in the volume of an activity or program. A prime example is after-school or student support services that employ physical plant for time periods after regular working hours. Regular working hour utility costs are relatively fixed; however, the use of buildings after this time means higher utility rates based on hours used.
6. Marginal Cost—Costs incurred for providing one more unit of a good or service. For example, adding one more student to a classroom.
7. Average Cost—Costs obtained by dividing the full costs associated with the production of a good or service, or activity or program by the number of individuals served. One example might be a tutoring program. For this instance, the total costs of the program are divided by the number of participating students.

As can be seen from these basic definitions, the measurement of costs is clearly difficult. However, the goal here is to simply highlight the ways in which costs can be understood and how these definitions can help budget managers more fully grasp the nuances of cost analysis and forecasting.

How do expenditures differ from costs? Most educators fail to recognize the subtle difference between the two terms and, as a result of this misunderstanding, view them as synonyms of one another. However, expenditures specifically refer to the amount of money spent on resources. For example, personnel represents an expenditure since there is a set amount of money allocated to ensuring there are resources, in the form of teachers, delivering instruction to students. Costs represent the price of the resource purchased by the school or school district official and begin to take into consideration the quality of the service.

Another example will better illustrate the difference between the two terms. An ineffective teacher represents an expenditure on a school's budget, and that expenditure captures the teacher's salary and benefits. However, the ineffective teacher also represents a cost to the school because he or she is not only costing the school the salary and benefits, but this teacher is also costing the school in the form of ineffective instruction (coaching time allocated to supporting the teacher, students assigned to this teacher underperforming academically, etc.). Later in this chapter, we will discuss the use of cost–benefit analyses to determine if an expenditure represents an effective and efficient allocation of resources.

P-12: Expenditures

Expenditures in P-12 public education typically fall into one of two categories (Alexander & Salmon, 1995, p. 86). These two categories are:

1. Total Expenditure: Total expenditure includes any cost covered by the school district. Specifically, total expenditure consists of current expenditure (see below), capital outlay projects, and any interest owed as a result of school district indebtedness. However, it does not include payments made to retire a loan's principal balance.
2. Current Expenditure: Current expenditure captures all of the costs associated with running the school district for a school year. It includes costs for administration, instruction, clerical services, health benefits, transportation, food services, and maintenance and operations. The current expenditure of a school district is captured in its total program allocation or the school district's annual budget.

Every school district is required, by law, to make its proposed budget publicly accessible before it is voted on by the local school board as well as once the budget is approved. A typical allocation of costs for a school district is presented in Table 3.4.

When analyzing the data presented in Table 3.4, it is important to note that there is a not a lot of "discretionary" money in public education. Almost 80% of a typical school district's expenditures cover personnel costs (instruction plus support services plus administration). A vast majority of the remaining budget is allocated to all of the other goods and services associated with running a school district.

The process of developing a school district budget includes a number of different steps. These points are summarized in Table 3.5. The budgetary development process described in Table 3.5 addresses the steps that must be taken to prepare a budget for the 2014–2015 school year.

The point documented in Table 3.5 is that the budgetary process is built upon anticipated revenues and costs. As the actual school year unfolds, the anticipated numbers may prove to be inaccurate. For example, student enrollment figures may turn out to be wrong. If the actual student enrollment figures come in significantly lower than the projected figures, then school district officials are faced with the possibility of having to cut personnel. If, on the other hand, the student enrollment figures come in higher than anticipated,

Table 3.4 Average School District Budget Allocation

Expenditure Category	Expenditure (%)
Instruction	62.9
Support services	7.5
Administration	7.6
Operations and maintenance	10.0
Transportation	4.5
Food services and other	7.5

Note: NCES, 2010.

Table 3.5   Preparation Work for a School District Budget

Timeline	Task	Description
Fall 2013	Program review	School leaders assess current program expenditures and the benefit associated with each cost. Certain programs could be discontinued if it is determined that the cost exceeds the benefit to the school district. If it is decided to discontinue a program, that would not take effect until the 2014–2015 fiscal year.
Fall 2013	Enrollment projections	Student enrollments represent the major revenue source for school districts. As a result, district leaders work to accurately anticipate future enrollments by examining birth rates, actual enrollment figures, and retention rates (this will be discussed in greater detail later).
Fall 2013	Expenditure projections	Another step in collecting all of the requisite data to develop a preliminary budget is for district leaders to identify expenditure projections for the upcoming fiscal year.
Spring 2014	School board workshops	With all of projections related to revenues (enrollment), program reviews, and expenditures district leaders begin to work with the elected school board. These workshops are focused on educating the board members on the budgetary process, discussing the projected fiscal solvency of the school district, and deciding the direction of the school district for the upcoming school year.
Spring 2014	Preliminary budget	With the input from the school board, school district leaders take the data collected related to program review, enrollment projections, and expenditure projections to develop a preliminary budget.
Spring 2014	Review/revise preliminary budget	The preliminary budget is then shared with all stakeholders (school level administrators, teacher association, parents, etc.) to seek input. The input can result in revisions to the preliminary budget to better capture the desires of the stakeholders.
May 2014	Present final budget to school board	By May, roughly two months before the budget goes into effect, school leaders present the final version of the budget to the school board. The school board can approve it as it stands, solicit additional information, or require revisions.
June 2014	Adoption of final budget	Once the school board is comfortable with the school district budget, it holds a public vote to adopt it. Once a positive vote to adopt the proposed budget is passed, the budget is approved and then goes into effect July 1, 2014.

Source: Cox, Weiler, & Cornelius, 2013, p. 62.

then school district officials have to add teachers after the start of the school year. Neither option is ideal.

How do school district and school building leaders plan for unanticipated costs? It is important to realize that there are two types of unanticipated costs: internal and external. Examples of internal unanticipated expenditures include the copier in the high school breaking down, an exceptionally high number of job-related injuries, a sudden spike in gas prices, or the roof of the elementary school gymnasium collapsing. Examples of external unanticipated costs include a state-imposed rescission (where the state takes back a portion of its allocation from the local school districts mid-school year due to tax revenue shortfalls at the state level) or unfunded mandates (school districts are required to adhere to a statute but receive no funding to do so).

School district and school building officials have a responsibility to spend each year's budget on the students in the building during that school year. However, these same leaders have a responsibility to keep sufficient money in reserve to be able to cover unanticipated expenses, either internal or external ones. It may seem like these two responsibilities are polar opposites, but a well-trained leader will be able to effectively adhere to both expectations. The following steps address basic strategies related to planning for unanticipated costs:

1. Cash Reserve: Every budget must keep a certain portion of its allocation in reserve for unanticipated expenditures. How much? That, ultimately, depends upon the practices within each school district and state law (e.g., in Alabama, school leaders are required to keep one-twelfth of the total program in reserve). However, typically, principals and school district leaders keep between 7 and 10% of the total program in reserve.

2. Spend Down Cash Reserve: As the school year advances, the cash reserve fund should be spent to ensure that the total allocation for the school year is spent on the students that school year.

3. Know Different Budgetary Fund Requirements: Some funds offer school district and school building leaders a greater degree of flexibility while other funds have specific requirements related to how they are to be spent that must be followed. Leaders must know the requirements associated with the different budget categories.

4. Don't Forget to Ask: This final principle applies mostly to building-level principals. When facing an unanticipated expenditure, they should not forget to ask others for help. For example, if the middle school has to have all of the doors rekeyed, it would be appropriate to ask the person in charge of maintenance to help with that expenditure. Every little amount helps take pressure off of the reserve fund.

Finally, related to costs, school district and building leaders are encouraged to develop their own philosophy related to creating and managing a budget and approving or rejecting expenditure requests. Ideally, your philosophy will include a commitment to spending most of the dollars each year in a fiscally conservative manner as well as a commitment to remaining as flexible as possible with public funds. The budget philosophy and state laws and/or regulations will detail how much money you will keep in reserve.

Prior to ending this section on P-12 expenditures, a final question must be posed. Does money matter? This single question has commanded an extensive amount of commentary from scholars, policymakers, and laypeople. Some scholars have argued that money does not correlate with student achievement (Coleman et al., 1966; Hanushek, 1989) while others have refuted such studies and established that there is a correlation between expenditures and student achievement (Hedges, Laine, & Greenweld, 1994).

Does an increase in expenditures ensure an increase in student achievement? Not necessarily. For additional funds to lead to an increase in student achievement, the new dollars have to be spent appropriately—the ultimate purpose and goal of this book is to help aspiring P-12 budget managers to know how to oversee public funds appropriately and effectively. However, it should be stressed here that additional dollars to P-12 education are always a welcome remedy to better provide all students with an adequate access to knowledge.

COST–BENEFIT ANALYSIS

P-12 administrators must be able to determine the effectiveness of expenditures, and one way to do so is through a cost–benefit analysis. An effective cost–benefit analysis, based on accurate data, empowers the budget manager and other decision-makers to:

• determine if the proposed expenditure is financially prudent and
• provide a basis for comparing expenditures.

These two benefits to a cost–benefit analysis cannot be overstated. Budget managers should constantly assess the appropriateness of existing expenditures and ask if there is a less expensive expenditure that would produce a similar benefit. For example, if a middle school invested $12,000 annually into a character education program, how would the budget manager for this school determine if this program was more effective than one that cost only $8,000 annually? The first step is to quantify the benefit gained as a result of the character education program.

Quantifying benefit in education is a bit of a challenge. However, prior to adopting a character education program, the leadership team at the middle school should have identified goals for the program. For example, was the aim of the character education program to reduce discipline referrals? Increase student attendance? Increase academic performance? All of these goals are quantifiable and allow the budget manager to run a cost–benefit analysis. This analysis could use a number of different formulas. For example, if the budget manager could report the analysis as a ratio (benefit–cost ratio):

$$\text{Benefit–Cost Ratio} = \text{Benefit/Cost.}$$

Or, the budget manager could report the analysis in the form of a net benefit:

$$\text{Net Benefit} = \text{Benefit} - \text{Cost.}$$

If the benefit of the character education program was measured in a reduction of 341 referrals from the year before its introduction and the year it was introduced to the student body, then the benefit–cost ratio would equal 341/12,000 (the cost of the program), or 0.028. If a second middle school was using the less expensive character education program and saw a reduction in referrals (realizing that we are failing to control for a myriad of other variables) of 89 then the benefit–cost ratio would be 0.011. A comparison of the two benefit–cost ratios suggests that the first school saw more benefit from the more expensive character education program than the second school with the less expensive program. Budget managers could also use the net benefit equation to perform a cost–benefit analysis.

It should be noted that with the passage of time, the benefit of an expenditure will either increase or decrease and a thorough cost–benefit analysis will capture the long-term impact of the expenditure. For example, it stands to reason that the reduction of discipline referrals will eventually flat line at both schools since there will always be a certain number of discipline referrals in a given year, regardless of the character education program that is adopted. As a result, with the passage of time the benefit of the character education program will decline since the reduction in discipline referrals will decline.

Cost–benefit analyses are effective tools at ensuring that current expenditures are producing the greatest possible benefit for the organization given the cost of the resource. As P-12 budget managers oversee budgets and accounts, they should look to run cost–benefit analyses to verify that limited public dollars are being effectively spent to produce the greatest possible benefit for students within the system.

ACCURATELY FORECASTING AND FORECASTING ACCURACY: COST CONSIDERATIONS

In the forecasting of costs, much like the forecasting of revenues, the same basic tenets apply. As noted previously, external and internal forces can have an effect on the cost and expenditure structures of schools and school districts. We also stressed the importance of accurate forecasting of revenues, and the same logic applies to the forecasting of costs.

Additionally, the study of multiple scenarios where worst- and best-case scenarios are considered applies to anticipating costs. While forecasting in general requires valid and appropriate data and providing reasonable estimates, the budget manager should provide cost forecasts that, unlike revenue, include scenarios where costs are higher than expected. In other words, the forecasting of revenues often requires conservative forecasts to make sure that budget decisions do not outstrip actual revenues. Conversely, cost forecasts should anticipate higher total in their calculations within reason.

Once again, we feel it is important to underscore that fact that it is not unusual for forecasts to be off by a reasonably small amount. However, even under the best conditions forecasts are limited by environmental instability, and hence, certain events may not be predicted accurately. Still, and for the most part, good forecasting can often provide a needed buffer against internal and external variability.

CONCLUSION

Revenues represent the foundation, or the lifeblood, of public P-20 education. They drive all of the expenditures and programs in P-20 education, and, for this reason, aspiring budget managers must have a foundational understanding of the origins of revenues and how to properly forecast revenues for each budget year cycle. In addition, expenditures represent the allocation of existing revenues to enhance the educational opportunities of students within the school or school district. As a result, budget managers should also demonstrate a clear understanding of the different expenditures in a P-12 school or school district budget. The understanding of revenues and expenditures allows budget managers to maximize the potential benefit of each dollar and, ultimately, provide all students with a meaningful educational experience.

GUIDING QUESTIONS

The following questions address many of the key concepts covered in chapter 3. Readers should be able to answer these questions upon completing the chapter:

1. How is the calculation of revenues in public education unique?
2. How are costs different from expenditures? Please provide examples of these differences.

3. How have the major revenue/expenditure categories in public education changed? Why?
4. How are a school district's mission statement, vision statement, goals, and strategic plan related to revenue and expenditure patterns and reliance?

ADDITIONAL READING

Those readers desiring additional information on the concepts addressed in chapter 3 should consult the following:

Brutless, G. (Ed.). 1996. *Does money matter? The effect of school resources on student achievement and adult success.* Washington, DC: Brookings Institution Press.

Levin H. M., & P. J. McEwan. 2001. *Cost-effectiveness analysis: Methods and applications* (2nd ed.). Thousand Oaks, CA: Sage Publications.

Monk, D. H., & B. O. Brent. 1997. *Raising money for education: A guide to the property tax.* Thousand Oaks, CA: Corwin Press.

Odden, A. R., & L. O. Picus. 2014. *School finance: A policy perspective* (5th ed.). Boston, MA: McGraw Hill. (Pay particular attention to chapters 6 and 8.)

EXERCISES

Exercise 1: Attendance Trends

In Table 3.6, readers will find the enrollment figures, by grade level, for a small school district over the past nine school years. Please note that the

Table 3.6 Enrollment History

	School Year								
Grade	2003–2004	2004–2005	2005–2006	2006–2007	2007–2008	2008–2009	2009–2010	2010–2011	2011–2012
K	100	132	100	130	125	155	148	155	150
1	110	114	145	121	146	129	159	140	140
2	119	111	120	146	127	132	135	156	155
3	126	111	120	123	143	125	137	143	156
4	110	124	127	123	123	131	134	143	143
5	116	131	134	136	116	121	137	132	146
6	163	120	121	138	145	126	129	148	139
7	140	158	121	127	148	146	133	141	153
8	158	140	166	126	131	146	142	130	134
9	139	156	141	163	119	135	132	146	139
10	105	133	156	128	140	114	125	125	137
11	105	97	120	130	118	130	117	110	115
12	100	101	92	112	115	115	121	99	97
Total	1,591	1,635	1,663	1,703	1,696	1,705	1,749	1,768	1,804

shaded cells serve to remind students of finance and budgeting that from one school year to the next the same group of students move to the next grade For example, in 2003–2004 school year (SY) there were 100 kindergarten students and in the 2004–2005 SY there were 114 first grade students. As a result, this group of students increased by 14 student in one year.

1. Based exclusively on the data reported in the table, predict the enrollment figures, by grade level, for this small school district. As you work on estimating enrollment figures for the 2012–2013 SY, determine a realistic addition or attrition rate for all groups of students as they move toward twelfth grade. In addition, anticipate an enrollment figure for Kindergarten for the 2012–2013 SY.

	School Year
Grade	2012–2013
K	
1	
2	
3	
4	
5	
6	
7	
8	
9	
10	
11	
12	
Total	

2. As you analyze the data in Table 3.6, you should see enrollment trends. Identify both the positive and negative enrollment trends you have noted based on the data reported in Table 3.6.
3. As you analyze the data reported in Table 3.6, what questions do you have? What would you like a better explanation of to understand what is actually occurring in the school district?
4. Assuming one student full-time equivalency (FTE) in this state is worth $8,000 (the amount of money the school district receives for each full-time student, first through twelfth grades, from the state), where could school district officials make the most impact on the school district's total program (or annual budget)? What would you propose doing to either increase enrollment or decrease attrition? How much more money do you anticipate the school district would receive?

Exercise 2: Actual Student Enrollment

One of the challenges with budgeting for public education is that revenue numbers are based on student count projections on July 1 of each year (the start of the fiscal year). However, school district officials do not know the actual student population for the school district until after the official student count.[4] So, states begin providing school districts funds at the start of a new fiscal year based on projected student count numbers, but the actual number of students being educated in any particular school district is not known until the start of the school year. As a result, school district revenues can be adjusted (the total program could either increase or decrease) by the state after the student count is completed. The data presented in Table 3.7 are from a school district that had built a budget around a projected student count of 5,280 but the actual number after the October 1 count stood at 5,509.

1. Determine the total student count for this school district based on the following components:
   a. The state funds only 58% of kindergarten.
   b. There are no half-time students.
   c. There are 57 students with disabilities enrolled in the school district's pre-K program, and the state funds these students at 0.5 of an FTE.
2. How much of a difference is there between the actual student count and the adjusted student count (after the work you did for 1)?
3. If an FTE in this state was $8,000, how much more/less money is the school district positioned to receive from the state?
4. How would you account for these adjustments to promote student achievement?

Table 3.7   Student Head Count

Grade	Student Count
Kindergarten	450
1	420
2	465
3	468
4	429
5	438
6	417
7	459
8	402
9	417
10	411
11	395
12	338
Total	5,509

Exercise 3: School-Level Student Enrollment Projections

An elementary school in a student-based budgeting (SBB) school district[5] had a student count of 272 in one school year. This increased to 319 students in the next school year. The elementary school's budget is presented in Table 3.8.

1. Determine the budget for this elementary school. How much money is left over?
2. What would happen to the budget if the school did not experience growth?
3. What would happen to the budget if the school district had not been able to pass the mill levy override?
4. What are the implications of your answers to items 2 and 3?
5. How could this school use the remaining money to benefit student achievement?

Exercise 4: Computing a Mill

Determining a district's mill levy rate:

School district's budget from property tax: $2,500,000
The school district's net assessed value (NAV): $100,000,000

1. How many mills will the county have to levy on the homeowners to provide the school district with its funds?

Table 3.8   Student Count at the School Level

Revenues		Expenses		
Budget Allocation	Budget Amount ($)	Budget Allocation	Budget Amount ($)	Total
SBB allocation	1,173,220			
Carryover from previous SY	6,300			
Mill levy allocation	73,706			
Mill levy staffing allocation	63,951			
		Contingency reserve		
		Operating budget		
		Staffing budget	923,077	
		Additional days for classified	4,633	
		Hire a new teacher	41,306	
		IB coordinator	25,045	
		Spanish tutor	7,600	
		Intervention coordinator	25,045	
		G/T teacher	6,261	

What is a mill levy?

A mill levy is a 0.1% tax on the NAV of each property.

Complete the following chart:

Mill Levy		Percent		Decimal
	=		=	

Mill levy on personal homeowner:

Your home is worth: $300,000

Assessed value rate for personal homeowners in Colorado: 7.96%

1. What is the taxable portion of your home?
2. The school district mill levy rate is 27.773. How much do you pay in taxes to support your local school district?
3. What if that rate were 27.77 instead of 27.773?
4. What is the power of the 0.003 mills?
5. When and for what reasons would a school district include a sunset, or an end date, on a proposed mill levy override?

Exercise 5: Full-Time Equivalency Allocation

Name of the school: Forging Tomorrow's Executives Middle School

Student population: 1,058 students

Sixth grade = 365 students

Seventh grade = 364 students

Eighth grade = 339 students

Core classes: Language Arts, Math, Science, Social Science, and Physical Education. (All students must take all five core classes.)

Teacher schedule: Each teacher teaches five classes and has one planning period. The final period (since FTEMS is on a seven-period schedule) is either team planning time or duty assignments.

Target class size: Ideally, each class will have between 20 and 25 students.

Elective Courses	Student Requests
Spanish (eighth grade only)	53
French (eighth)	29
Latin (eighth)	18
Algebra (seventh only)	101
Geometry (eighth only)	98
Beginning Art (sixth only)	110
Intermediate art	182
Advanced art	143
Beginning band (sixth only)	107

Elective Courses	Student Requests
Intermediate band	87
Advanced band	76
Beginning choir (sixth only)	68
Intermediate choir	81
Advanced choir	76
Beginning technical education (sixth only)	80
Intermediate technical education	73
Advanced technical education	53
Beginning agricultural education (sixth only)	80
Intermediate agricultural education	101
Advanced agricultural education	60
Beginning family and consumer science (FACS) (sixth only)	81
Intermediate FACS	103
Advanced FACS	60
Sixth grade rotation	200

Directions: Use the information provided earlier:

1. Determine the number of full-time equivalencies (FTEs) required to staff this school (an FTE equals one full-time teacher) from the principal's perspective. Do not worry about the feasibility of finding one teacher that can teach French, Latin, and Spanish—assume that anything is possible.
2. Determine the number of FTEs required to staff this school from the school district's perspective.
3. How could you use staffing allocations to better meet the individual needs of low performing students?

NOTES

1. While the nuance of this notion is outside of the scope of the current chapter, readers can obtain further information on this topic from Winston (1999) and Parkin (2010).

2. Some states allow school districts to add individual taxes based on needs and abilities. However, that freedom to add taxes is somewhat challenging as most of these opportunities must be put to a public vote, which is costly and does not always yield a vote of approval.

3. Per pupil operating revenue is also referred to as the per pupil expenditure.

4. Most states require school districts to conduct a student count on or around October 1 of the school year. The use of average daily membership or average daily attendance is gaining popularity in a number of states due to the greater accuracy these approaches at counting student populations offer state leaders.

5. By definition, student-based budgeting provides the building principal with the entire budget for the school and entrusts that individual to account for all of the budgetary requirements, including personnel salaries and benefits.

Chapter 4

Basics of Financial Ratio Analysis

The foundational elements of financial ratios and how to use them are the main foci of this chapter. A ratio, by definition, is a quantifiable way of representing the relationship between two measurements. In the fiscal administration of schools and school districts, ratios can provide much needed information and evidence about the financial standing and fiscal viability of the school district. To help frame this in the day-to-day activities of P-12 budget managers, this chapter covers only the most typical ratios used in public education and provides a step-by-step approach for understanding how to analyze and interpret the data conveyed by financial ratios, as well as their limitations.

FINANCIAL RATIOS

Broadly speaking, financial ratios provide information about four areas of fiscal administration and budgeting:

1. Resource liquidity and flexibility
2. Debt capacity, leverage, and management
3. Asset performance and management
4. How an institution uses and obtains its funds (Chabotar, 1989; Prager, McCarthy, & Sealy, 2002)

These four areas arguably compose the major financial structures of a school district. By employing financial ratios across these areas it is possible to obtain a broad, summative understanding of a school district's fiscal standing. As required by statute, school districts publish an extensive summary of the total program, or annual budget. This document obviously varies from school district to school district due to a number of factors, including: specific state requirements, size of the school district, the existence of a voter-approved mill levy override, and the number of outstanding bonds. This detailed school district budget document will include all of the data required to conduct the ratios discussed throughout this chapter.

USES OF FINANCIAL RATIOS

There are, generally speaking, four specific questions that should guide the use and interpretation of financial ratios:

1. Are resources sufficient and flexible enough to support the mission?
2. Does asset performance and management support the strategic direction?
3. Do operating results indicate the institution is living within available resources?
4. Is debt managed strategically to advance the mission? (Prager, McCarthy, & Sealy, 2002, p. 5)

By considering these four questions, P-12 decision-makers are better able to determine the best ways in which to allocate resources to meet institutional objectives, goals, and mission. Indeed, Chabotar (1989) suggested that ratio analysis provides a means for answering these questions. This is because financial ratios provide a gauge, or metric, for understanding whether the leaders of the school district are positioned to answer each of these questions in the positive. Even if decision-makers answer these questions in the negative, financial ratios can help them determine where problems and obstacles exist.

In addition, financial ratios provide information to external stakeholders. Especially in the state, policymakers are introducing more complex accountability, performance-based, and oversight mechanisms, which are often accompanied by requests for increased data and information (Hillman, Tandberg, & Gross, 2014; McLendon, Hearn, & Deaton, 2006; Tandberg & Hillman, 2014). Financial ratios allow school district officials to review these more complex accounting mechanisms in a way that stakeholders will better understand.

Financial ratios are a simple way to provide information regarding the fiscal standing of a school district and a quick measure of whether the school district is employing it resources appropriately related to its stated mission, vision, and goals. However, an important cautionary note is required here: while these measures afford a quick snapshot look at a school district's finances, as with any and all other data used for decision-making, financial ratios should be understood in context and with appropriate restraint.

Now that the fundamental uses of financial ratios have been presented, the focus of the next section is on the types of financial ratios P-12 budget managers are likely to encounter.

TYPES AND INTERPRETATION OF FINANCIAL RATIOS

There exist a multitude of financial ratios across finance and financial management. However, for public school districts, only a few of these matter a great deal for gauging fiscal standing. In order to employ financial ratios, the P-12 budget manager needs to determine which ratio to use. Next, he or she must know where to obtain the required values. Finally, the P-12 budget manager needs to know how to interpret the results of the calculation. In the following sections, the process related to financial ratios is outlined in a step-by-step manner.

Drawing upon a number of sources (Chabotar, 1989; Finkler et al., 2013; Fischer et al., 2004; Prager, McCarthy, & Sealy, 2002), the following sections introduce the basic elements of financial ratio analysis by separating them into four general areas. While a number of alternatives exist to the ratios presented here (see Prager, McCarthy, & Sealy, 2002; Fischer et al., 2004), these provide a foundational understanding of financial ratios for the aspiring P-12 budget manager.

Liquidity Ratios

The goal of liquidity ratios is to determine the financial strength of an institution's cash flow. In addition, liquidity ratios measure a school district's cash flow against its short-term obligations. These ratios rely upon the current assets and liabilities, or quickly cash-convertible assets and quickly due liabilities, or liabilities due within a year's time.

In most cases, current assets and liabilities are clearly indicated within a school district's annual budget report. The typical assets and liabilities included in the calculation of liquidity ratios are identified in Table 4.1. In the

Table 4.1   Typical Current Asset and Liabilities

Current Asset Types	*Current Liability Types*
Cash and cash equivalents (checking balances, petty cash, etc.)	Accounts payable
Accounts/notes receivable	Deferred revenues
Short-term investments	Current debt service
Inventories	Current capital lease service
Prepaid expenses	Accrued leave (unused leave balances)

instance that the required data are not reported separately, an understanding of the local context, coupled with technical know-how, comes into play. The P-12 budget manager can always request for information that is not readily apparent on financial reports produced for public consumption.

As a quick aside, it is important to note the distinction between restricted and unrestricted assets and liabilities. Similar to restricted and unrestricted revenues discussed later in this chapter, assets and liabilities that fall into restricted categories are limited in their use. That is to say, restricted assets and liabilities are only available and payable with monies from the specific funding sources. An example of this point of restricted assets would be title funds from the federal government. These dollars come with specific requirements on how they can and cannot be spent.

The most common of liquidity ratios is referred to as the *current ratio* (Chabotar, 1989, p. 193; Finkler et al., 2013). The current ratio is illustrated in the following formula:

Current Ratio = Unrestricted Current Assets/Unrestricted Current Liabilities.

The word "current" indicates the inclusion of assets that are quickly transformable, within a year or less, to cash. A similar notion applies to current liabilities. These are expenses that are required to be paid within a year. Typically, the goal should be to maintain a *current ratio* of 2:1 or simply 2. What this indicates is that for every dollar of current liabilities, the institution has \$2 in current assets. Anything much lower than the 2:1 ratio is likely to draw unwanted, and negative, attention from creditors. In addition, a ratio lower than 2:1 could signal that cash reserves are being depleted (Chabotar, 1989; Finkler et al., 2013).

While it might seem like a good idea to have a higher ratio in this case, a current ratio that is higher than 2 implies that the approach for determining and forecasting current cash needs is overly conservative. An excessively conservative budget management strategy could result in a loss of investment income if current assets are failing to earn interest for the school district. While the current ratio provides a quick measure of liquidity, it can also mask cash flow problems when an institution is able to transfer funds from other areas.

The next measure of liquidity is called the *quick ratio*. This ratio does a better job of accounting for the role of inventories in the school district since it separates these assets from *Unrestricted Current Assets*. In order to measure the quick ratio, the following equation is used:

Quick Ratio = Unrestricted Current Assets-Inventories/Unrestricted Current
              Liabilities.

As this ratio takes a more conservative approach to the estimation of current assets, a ratio of 1:1 or 1 is acceptable. Again, the larger the ratio, the more important it becomes to examine cash forecasting assumptions, discussed later in the text, to make sure that funds are not sitting idle. Conversely, if the ratio is closer to zero, this could suggest a real cash flow problem, and an examination of current spending or resource allocation decisions should take place.

A third liquidity ratio, referred to as the *available funds ratio*, is a more conservative measure of a school district's liquidity. The available funds ratio limits the inclusion of current assets to cash and short-term investments and is represented in the following equation:

$$\text{Available Funds Ratio} = \text{Cash and Short-Term Investments/Unrestricted Current Liabilities.}$$

In the available funds ratio, only assets deemed to be liquid are included in the numerator. Given that this ratio is even more conservative than the quick ratio, it is acceptable for it to be as low as 0.75:1 or 0.75 cents of highly liquid assets to every dollar of current liabilities. Using this extremely conservative measure allows a P-12 budget manager to truly understand the cash position of the school district or school since the included assets are limited to those that are near cash equivalents (Chabotar, 1989).

Operating Performance Ratios

The ratios included in this category typically measure the flexibility of a school district's resources, or gauge if a school district's budget is "living within available resources" (Prager, McCarthy, & Sealy, 2002, p. 22). In order to obtain the necessary information for calculation of these ratios, the P-12 budget manager should look to the *statement of revenues, expenses, and changes in net assets* or the *statement of activities* from a school district budget.

Typical operating revenues, expenditures, and nonoperating revenues are presented in Table 4.2. However, P-12 budget managers should be aware that "variations in account practices across [organizations] could result in the same expenditure item being grouped into different categories" (Toutkoushian, 2001, p. 17). Not only does this hold true for expenditures, but the same could be applied to revenue variables. Therefore, the information reported in Table 4.2 should be used only as a guide for understanding the respective components of operating performance ratios.

A reminder of the information covered in chapter 3: revenues can be categorized into restricted and unrestricted categories. For the P-12 budget

Table 4.2 General Operating Categories and Included Elements by Functional Classification

Operating Revenues	Operating Expenses	Nonoperating Revenues
Local property taxes	Personnel—teaching	Gifts
State taxes (income, sales, and/or lottery)	Personnel—administration	Foundations
Federal income taxes	Personnel—support staff	Investment income
Grants/contracts	Operations and maintenance	
Sales and services	Transportation	
	Food services	
	Other	

Source: NCES, 2010.

manager, this means maintaining clear oversight of which funds are available for general use and which are restricted to only specific uses. Because restricted funds (revenues or assets), and often any income derived from these funds, can only be used for certain purposes, using these numbers in the calculation of both liquidity and operating ratios should take into account the special character of restricted fund and asset classifications.

Two general ratios employed to measure operating results and flexibility include the *net operating ratio* and *expenditures by program or function ratio*. The *net operating ratio* is usually calculated using some combination of net operating revenues divided by total revenues, or total unrestricted revenues (Chabotar, 1989; Fischer et al., 2004, p. 133; Prager, McCarthy, & Sealy, 2002), and takes the form:

Net Operating Ratio = Operating Revenues–Operating Expenses/Total (Unrestricted) Revenues.

When interpreting this ratio, a general approach is to determine if the ratio returns a result that is above or below 1.0. If the result is below 1.0, this indicates a deficit. If it is above 1.0, this indicates a surplus (Chabotar, 1989). An important caveat is necessary at this juncture.

For public school districts, it is not unusual to show an operating loss. This is because, as noted in chapter 3, operating revenues are decidedly connected to those revenues derived from the general operations. In public school districts, part of the total program comes from state support. However, the state contribution to a local school district does not come in one lump sum. Rather, the state issues a monthly allotment to each school district. In addition, employees are paid monthly, and bills arrive at the school district's central office on a monthly basis. Hence, if the calculation just presented is used, it will always return a ratio of less than 1.0.

A way to get around this limitation is for school district officials to present a ratio of total revenues to total expenditures (Chabotar, 1989) as follows:

Revised Net Operating Ratio = Total Expenditures/Total Revenues.

To illustrate, assume that public school district officials calculate the difference between the operating revenues and operating expenditures and the result is −$244,796. If this sum is compared to an operating revenue of $780,743, then the *net operating ratio* would be equal to −0.313, suggesting that the school district consistently has fund deficits. If, instead, the comparison is made between total expenditures and total revenues, then the example, including nonoperating revenues, would result in a situation where, for example, total expenses equal $1,025,539 and total revenues include the $780,743 of operating revenues and $324,169 of nonoperating revenues, the ratio changes to approximately 1.08.

Clearly, this second calculation is a better indicator of the financial net operations of a public school district. Additionally, it should be underscored that if the ratio is below 1.0 for one year, this is not necessarily a problem, assuming the school district has cash reserves to cover the deficit. Concerns should arise, however, around a trend where the net operating ratio is less than 1.0 for more than a couple of consecutive years, if deficits are characteristic of more than two of the most recent five years, or if there is a deficit larger than 10% of total revenue in any single year or more (Chabotar, 1989, p. 199).

The next operating ratio to consider is the *expenditures by program or function ratio*. As will be noted in chapter 10, coupling the expenditure by program or function ratio with the organization's strategic planning, fiscal administration, and budget alignment provides a clear measure of the school district's priorities over and above any plan. The ratio is calculated using the following information (Chabotar, 1989, p. 198):

Program or Function Ratio = Expenditures by Program or Function/
Total Expenditures.

Rather than provide a strict range of values, this ratio measures the total resources expended on a particular program or function. This type of ratio is especially useful for P-12 budget managers who wish to understand how resources of a school district are being expended. This ratio is also useful in helping to determine the relative position that stated goals and objectives maintain in allocation decisions. For example, if the total budget for a school is $1,025,539 and the costs associated with a remedial reading intervention program are equal to $17,237, then the percentage of the budget dedicated to the remedial reading intervention effort is less than 2% (1.68%).

It could be argued that if the remedial reading intervention program is considered a strategic priority, the school budget allocation appears to be insufficient. What is the optimal percent of a budget that should be dedicated to an educational priority? Unfortunately, there is no clear answer to that question. The P-12 budget manager will take into consideration the fact that over 80% of a school or school district budget is automatically allocated to fixed costs in the form of personnel salaries and benefits. When other set expenditures, such as transportation, supplies, maintenance, and utilities, are considered, the P-12 budget manager is left with a paltry amount of discretionary funding. As a result, the allocation of 2–5% of a total budget could actually represent a significant commitment on the part of the school or school district toward a particular program or effort.

Debt and Solvency Ratios

The next set of ratios to be considered are those related to the debt structure of a school district, and the P-12 budget manager's ability to preserve the solvency of a budget, or to pay its bills as they come due. The first ratio, *debt–equity ratio*, provides a test of a school district's ability to access long-term credit and debt markets based on its current debt levels and expendable net assets (Fischer et al., 2004, p. 133; Prager, McCarthy, & Sealy, 2002, p. 23). Generally speaking, the *debt–equity ratio* takes the form:

$$\text{Debt–Equity Ratio} = \text{Expendable Net Assets/Long-Term Debt.}$$

This happens where the numerator for the calculation comprises asset categories that include only the expendable, both restricted and unrestricted, portion of net assets. The denominator in this case "includes all notes, bonds, and capital leases payable" (Prager, McCarthy, & Sealy, 2002, p. 24) that fall under *noncurrent liabilities*. An overview of regularly included assets and debt types is provided in Table 4.3.

When employing this measure of debt structure, there is no absolute "best" value. The measure instead can provide information regarding the sufficiency of expendable net assets to pay debt obligations as they come due. And while

Table 4.3   Regularly Included Asset and Debt Types

Expendable Net Assets	Long-Term Debt
Total program*	Bonds
Interest	Long-term debt
Additional revenue sources (i.e., vending)*	
Unrestricted assets	

*Indicates that the asset is restricted but expendable.

a ratio of 1:1 or higher suggests sufficient solvency, this may be too high or low based on factors specific to the school district. Still, P-12 budget managers should be wary of allowing this ratio to fall to far below the 1:1 ratio (Prager, McCarthy, & Sealy, 2002).

This is because a ratio that falls below the 1:1 threshold can signal to external stakeholders, including debt markets, that the school district is likely to have more difficulty being flexible and responding to adverse financial conditions. However, the ratio only provides a quick glimpse of the viability of an institution based on its debt structure. As with other ratios, it should be one piece, not the only piece, of information and should be examined for trends over time.

The next two ratios that constitute a measure of a school district's debt structure and solvency include the *debt-service ratio*, which focuses on revenues (Chabotar, 1989, p. 196; Finkler et al., 2013, p. 574), and the *debt-service burden ratio*, which focuses on expenditures (Prager, McCarthy, & Sealy, 2002, p. 28). The debt-service ratio seeks to provide a quick metric of the relationship between current debt service and revenues and is calculated as:

Debt-Service Ratio = Debt-Service/Total Revenues.

Similarly, the *debt-service burden ratio* seeks to understand the proportion of a school district's expenditures dedicated to servicing existing debt (Prager, McCarthy, & Sealy, 2002). The debt-service burden ratio employs the same numerator with the same information, but this time as a denominator uses total expenditures as a comparison such that:

Debt-Service Burden Ratio = Debt-Service/Total Expenditures.

Finkler et al. (2013, p. 575) and Chabotar (1989, p. 196) suggested that a good goal for the *debt-service ratio* is 8–10% of the school district's total program. In the case of a school, the goal should be similar, 8–10% of the annual budget. P-12 budget managers need to balance their duty to responsibly manage public funds in a fiscally prudent manner with their duty to spend these public dollars on the students that are currently in the school district. Extremes, either keeping too much money in reserve or spending every last penny before the end of the fiscal year, are dangerous and should be avoided.

Specifically, to work toward being debt-free, P-12 budget managers must aim to distinguish between "good debt" and "bad debt." For example, school district officials should be able to assume that a new school building will be operational for roughly 50 years. However, it is also safe to assume that in

25 years' time, the building will require a major renovation. This concept is typically referred to as the 25/50 rule. The debt required to overhaul the building to extend its usefulness and life would be considered "good debt."

P-12 budget managers should be aware of the trend in the debt-service burden ratio. It is not enough to take a single cross-section and assume that this is a good indicator of the school district's debt-service or debt-service burden. Indeed, it is an analysis of the trend in either of these measures that signals whether a school district has leveraged itself appropriately and if it has sufficient flexibility to fund new capital projects while servicing previous ones.

Source Ratios

While this section is called source ratios, the reality is that a single calculation exists for determining the role played by a certain part of the revenue for a school district. The *contribution ratio* is used to determine the proportion of a particular revenue component as compared to total expenditures and is measured in the following formula (Chabotar, 1989, p. 197):

Contribution Ratio = Source of Revenue/Total Expenditures.

This allows the P-12 budget manager to determine the ratio, or percentage of revenues, from a single source compared to total expenditures. For example, assume that the state's contribution to a rural school district's total program is equal to $3,113,710 and the school district's total budget is $10,255,390. Then the state contributes 30.4% to the school district's total program. In other words, about one-third of expenditures constitute tuition and fees. As can be seen, this metric can provide useful information regarding the trends in revenue dependence to cover institutional operating expenses.

Additionally, the contribution ratio can provide a sense of how a school district's revenue dependence tracks to expenses over time. This ratio can also show how changes in certain categories or sources have become more pronounced or have diminished as the external and internal environments respond to variability. While there exists little guidance around the proper ratios or proportions that P-12 budget managers should maintain, there are key points to consider, and these points are discussed here.

First, a goal should be to maintain revenue diversification so that changes in a single source do not have too severe an impact on the school district's overall revenue sources. Similar to investment portfolios, diversifying revenue reliance is sound fiscal practice.

Second, and related, should be maintaining flexibility. It becomes problematic if flexibility is compromised and reliance upon a single or couple of revenue sources is high. Indeed, a major concern in determining creditworthiness and fiscal sustainability for a school district is the ability to respond to a changing economic and political environment.

CAUTIONS ON FINANCIAL RATIO ANALYSIS

Before concluding this chapter, it is necessary to highlight a few cautions related to financial ratio analysis. First, a comprehensive decision-making process should employ financial ratios, as well as the school district's annual financial report, to understand the school district's position more fully. Omitting this from the decision-making process, or from any process where the goal is to gain more far-reaching knowledge of fiscal administration, is folly.

Second, though it has been mentioned over and over again in this chapter, the use of multiple years of data and trend analysis is crucial in applied budgeting and fiscal administration of schools and school districts. Moreover, using multiple years of data and trends can help guide P-12 budget managers to make clearer connections between financial ratio analysis and strategic plans and goals.

Third, it is almost never the case that a single ratio can provide sufficient information. Using multiple ratios over many years can help to alleviate some of the obscuring effects of using only one. Additionally, using multiple points of data, information, and metrics provides a solid foundation for decision-making that is interested in maintaining fiscal sustainability.

CONCLUSION

The goal of this chapter has been to provide new P-12 budget managers with some basic information regarding financial ratios and their analysis. Ideally, the content of this chapter has provided a foundational understanding of the primary elements and uses of financial ratio in the fiscal administration of schools and school districts. The discussion in this chapter has been limited to only those ratios that would likely hold the most relevance in the day-to-day operations of a school district.

GUIDING QUESTIONS

The following questions address many of the key concepts covered in chapter 4. Readers should be able to answer these questions upon completing the chapter:

1. Why do public school administrators overseeing budgets use ratios? What are some of the best uses of ratio analysis?
2. Explain some of the major advantages of the different types of ratios discussed in this chapter.
3. What are some cautions P-12 budget managers should consider when using ratio analysis? How does this relate to human judgment in the process?

ADDITIONAL READING

Those readers desiring additional information on the concepts addressed in chapter 4 should consult the following:

Baker, B. D., P. Green, & C. E. Richards. 2008. *Financing education systems.* Upper Saddle River, NJ: Pearson. (Please refer to chapters 11–15.)
Poston, Jr., W. K. 2011. *School budgeting for hard times: Confronting cutbacks and critics.* Thousand Oaks, CA: Corwin Press. (Please refer to chapter 4.)

EXERCISES

Using the data in the school district budget that you accessed in chapter 1, answer the following questions:

1. Using the financial statements from the school district budget report (the financial statement could be any of the reports included in the budget—debt service, total program, etc.—you choose), calculate the following liquidity ratios:
   a. Current ratio
   b. Quick ratio
   c. Available funds ratio
   Finally, briefly describe how each of these differs from one another.
2. Using the financial statements from the school district budget report (the financial statement could be any of the reports included in the budget—debt service, total program, etc.—you choose), calculate the following:
   a. Net operating ratio
   b. Program/function ratio for student aid expenditures
   c. Revised net operating ratio
   Finally, briefly discuss why the net operating ratio and revised net operating ratio would differ for a public college or university.

3. Using the financial statements from the school district budget report (the financial statement should be the debt-service report), calculate the following debt and solvency ratios:
   a. Debt-equity ratio
   b. Debt-service ratio
   c. Debt-service burden ratio
   Finally, briefly discuss what each of these ratios is measuring and how they differ.
4. A school district has the local energy company do an energy audit of all of its facilities. The audit recommends the following changes:
   - Light fixtures need to be changed and updated throughout the school district.
   - The boilers need to be replaced with units that have higher efficiency.
   - Solar heating needs to be installed to heat the swimming pool.
   - An automation system needs to be installed to control the heating and cooling of all buildings in the school district.

If these changes are made, the energy company guarantees that the school district would save $93,720 annually in charges paid to the company. The total cost to do all the work required is $3.97 million. Does it make sense to allocate $3.97 million for renovations? Assuming the school district is able to secure grant dollars, what would be the optimal ratio between grant dollars (through state and local entities) and school district contribution (which would be obtained through a bond)? Hint: ideally, the guaranteed savings would cover the bond payments.

Chapter 5

Forecasting, Accuracy, and Judgment

Forecasting is the practice of making predictions about a future state of affairs (Dunn, 2012; Stevenson, 2015). While there are many techniques for doing so, the basics of accurate forecasting require at least three factors: good data, good local contextual knowledge, and good analysts.[1]

First, the importance of good data should be self-evident to those with budgeting responsibilities. Good data provide the backbone for accurate forecasting, which assists in decision-making at all levels. Without good data, forecasts are unreliable. Therefore, P-12 budget managers involved in forecasting should know the data well.

Second, P-12 budget managers are often required to make predictions about the financial standing of the organization as well as to anticipate what might occur based on previous historical knowledge. This type of contextual information tends not to be taught in a classroom but rather is specific to the local conditions and organizational culture. In order for forecasting to be accurate and for P-12 budget managers to provide useful information, a detailed understanding of the organization's context is vital.

The final piece of accurate forecasting is good analysts. Accurate and useful forecasting requires a certain set of technical and analytical abilities. The goal of this chapter is to provide the reader with the knowledge to accurately forecast different P-12 budget factors, such as student enrollment or teacher attrition.

In this chapter we present forecasting foundations. After reading this chapter, students should be prepared to execute basic forecasting techniques. Students will also be exposed to the multiple strategies available to them, including linear, nonlinear, and expert judgment approaches to forecasting. Moreover, they will examine some of the limitations of forecasting and appropriate expectations around the uses of forecasting results. It is important to note that the techniques presented in this chapter, while setting the foundations for the exercises in chapter 3, extend well beyond the anticipation of costs and revenues. In fact, many of the techniques offered here can be used to anticipate an array of external influences on a P-12 budget.

EXPECTATIONS AND USES OF FORECASTING RESULTS

For the most part, forecasting should be seen as one more piece of information for decision-making. It can provide decision-makers with "what if" analyses that vary conditions in multiple scenarios (Rylee, 2011). The forecast can help decision-makers consider the consequences of multiple courses of action. It can also help buffer the school district or school against threats and opportunities that may arise. However, forecasting should not be seen as the only, or even the best, way to make decisions.

Forecasting should be one piece of information that takes into account possible scenarios, or future states of affairs, and incorporates local knowledge and analytical expertise. While forecasts can serve as a basis for decision-making, good forecasts include two essential realizations.

First, all forecasts will be off by some degree or dollar amount. The goal of forecasting is to get as close as possible to the true value based on good data, good local knowledge, and good technical expertise. When forecasts deviate a great deal from the actual value, it may be necessary to examine these variances and review the underlying assumptions going into the forecasting approach. Techniques for conducting variance analysis are covered in greater detail in chapter 7.

Second, all forecasts are subject to sudden and unexpected deviations based on unanticipated events. For example, the economic reverberations from the bursting of the housing bubble in 2008 eventually created a decrease in tax revenue for local school districts that, in turn, impacted educational appropriations and support. It is unlikely that this type of fluctuation would have been accounted for by forecasting models employing historical data, although some might argue that local knowledge and technical expertise should have accounted for this to some extent. Nonetheless, it is always important to note that these types of events result in massive variances between the forecasted and actual values even if the best data, analysts, and techniques are employed.

FORECASTING APPROACHES AND METHODS

Generally speaking there are three categories of forecasting approaches: averages, linear, and curvilinear. In this section, we will highlight the uses, advantages, and limitations of each. We will also provide a foray into the actual techniques. These techniques will be useful for the exercises included in chapter 3. Hence, in this section, we provide only basic examples. It is important to highlight that the use of forecasting techniques assumes that time-series data (data for multiple years, months, days, etc.) are available. It is the nature of time-series data that allows a P-12 budget manager to extrapolate from past events to possible future ones (Dunn, 2012). Let us now turn to the first approach of forecasting by averages.

Using Averages for Forecasting

This type of forecasting typically employs averages of historical data to predict future values. The benefit of using this forecasting technique is based on its dependence on historical information. The inclusion of data that fluctuate upward and downward means that the use of averages smoothens out any variability. It is also advantageous to use this method because averages tend to reflect the random variation of data. This means that the information provided by this technique can allow decision-makers to react to needed changes rather than simply minor variations (Finkler et al., 2013; Stevenson, 2015). In other words, small variations based on the smoothing of the data through the use of averages indicates that P-12 budget managers should pay close attention to large deviations and what these swings could mean for future decision-making.

While this technique readily lends itself to practical use because of its ease of both formulation and interpretation, some important limitations exist. First, the use of historical data and the "moving" part of the average shows that this technique can be very sensitive to the number of data points included in the forecast.[2] This is because when the moving average calculates each new forecast point, it picks up the most current period's data point and drops the oldest, or least current, period. This also means that each value is given equal weight.

Second, depending upon how many points are included from the most current to the least current, the forecasted value can vary considerably (Stevenson, 2015). In other words, if more data points are included from time periods further away from the present, the smoothing effect of past events becomes more pronounced, which is not always an accurate portrayal of future events. If a greater number of points are included from more recent periods, then the forecast will weight recent events more heavily. The point here is that budget managers should be aware of the trade-offs made when certain data or assumptions guide the forecast.

To make this more concrete, consider the fictional data set that we will use for the rest of the chapter and compare how different choices around data

Table 5.1 Fictional Data Set for Forecasting Student Enrollments

School Year	Number of Students	Weights Over 3 Years	Weights Over 5 Years
2001–2002	15,123		
2002–2003	16,345		
2003–2004	17,567		
2004–2005	18,789		
2005–2006	19,901		
2006–2007	20,123		0.10
2007–2008	21,456		0.15
2008–2009	22,000	0.15	0.20
2009–2010	23,678	0.35	0.25
2010–2011	24,922	0.50	0.30
Total Weight		**1.0**	**1.0**

inclusion change forecasts. We should highlight that here we use forecasting for calculating future student enrollments; however, all of the techniques presented here are fully applicable to revenues and expenditures. Using the data in Table 5.1, we will calculate a three-period, or three school years in this case, basic moving average and a five-period basic moving average for forecasting the expected number of students for period eleven. We will also move from the more basic moving average forecasting technique to weighted moving average and use some examples that compare the two techniques.

To carry out the forecasting average calculation, we will need a few pieces of information. Using Stevenson's (2015, p. 86) example, the following equation provides a basic framework for calculating a moving average:

$$\text{Forecast}_t = \text{Moving Average}_n = \frac{\sum_{i=1}^{n} A_i}{n}.$$

This happens when the forecast for the time period under consideration is equal to the moving average of a certain number of periods. The moving average is calculated by taking each value for the school years to be included (for our first example, the last three school years) and summing them together. Then this value is divided by the total number of school years included. This would indicate that the following equation for our dataset is correct:

$$F_{11} = MA_{3-period} = \frac{22,000 + 23,678 + 24,922}{3} = 23,533.3.$$

Hence, our forecasted number of students for the 2011–2012 school year based on a three-period moving average is 23,533.3. Now let's consider a five-period moving average example using the same data.

$$F_{11} = MA_{5-\text{period}} = \frac{20,123 + 21,456 + 22,000 + 23,678 + 24,922}{5} = 22,435.8.$$

As can be seen, the forecasted number of students based on a three-school year average, instead of a five-school year one, results in a lower forecast with a difference of 1,097.5 students. This difference in estimates using just two more school years of data shows two things. First, the inclusion of more data has impacted the forecast by what might be considered a large amount. This basic example should show how sensitive estimates are to the number of data points used as well as how distance from the present affects the forecast. In other words, this is why moving averages typically do not employ a ten or twenty period.

Second, local context about environmental factors and budget management/philosophy will often dictate how many years of data will be appropriate for use. It is, therefore, imperative that the assumptions going into the forecasting model and technique itself are understood clearly (Dunn, 2012).

Turning to weighted moving average, the basic premise is the same as the first technique with one exception—weights are assigned to time periods to indicate relative importance of some over others instead of simply dividing by the total number of included years. The advantage of this more advanced technique is that it assigns heavier weight to recent events that might impact the estimated value of some important variable. We should underscore that the weights used over the time-period must equal one (Stevenson, 2015). Using a similar equation as earlier, the weighted moving average calculation includes these weights as follows for three school years:

$$F_{11} = WMA_{3-\text{period}} = .15(22,000) + .35(23,678) + .50(24,922) = 24,048.3.$$

Doing the same for five school years, the equation is:

$$F_{11} = WMA_{5-\text{period}}$$
$$= .10(20,123) + .15(21,456) + .20(22,000) + .25(23,678) + .30(24,922)$$
$$= 23,026.8.$$

Once again, what becomes evident is that the method and assumptions that go into the forecasting approach and methodology employed impact future estimates. In the weighted example, the difference in the three- and five-school year estimates still sits at over 1,000 (1,021.5 to be exact [24048.3–23026.8 = 1,021.5]). As stated earlier, a benefit of this technique is that it explicitly sets weights to time periods so as to account for the relative importance of more recent events as compared to earlier ones while including information from dates that are further away from the present.

A primary limitation of this approach is that the choice of weights for each period of data included is rather subjective and may require multiple iterations to determine the appropriate weighting format (Stevenson, 2015). For example, a P-12 budget manager may experiment with past enrollment data to determine which weight distribution best predicts actual data by comparing the weighted forecasts, ex post facto, to the actual figures.

Two techniques for using moving averages to forecast future values have been briefly explained in this section. While we have provided two examples using three- and five-school year averages, P-12 budget managers should note that the number of years used in this type of forecasting approach is reliant upon what is considered appropriate based on context, local information, and data availability.

It is also important to highlight that forecasts can be extended for many time periods beyond the available data using the calculated averages as done earlier. Also, in the process of forecasting, data variations based upon seasonality, secular trends, and business cycles should be taken into account. That is, when variations are examined, large deviations from averages might be due to external, but well-known, factors such as those just noted (Dunn, 2012; Finkler et al., 2013).

Exponential Smoothing

As just noted, weighted averages allow for P-12 budget managers to explicitly assign importance to certain time periods when making forecasts. In exponential smoothing, a similar weighting occurs, but in this case the forecast is dependent upon the value of the previous period's forecast and a percentage of the forecasting error (Stevenson, 2015). In other words, rather than assign an explicit weight to each time period, this method allows the P-12 budget manager to smoothen out the next estimate by evenly spreading the weight using a constant percentage of the forecasting error from one time period to the next.

Because this method is closely related to understanding forecasting accuracy, in this section we only introduce the basic mechanics behind the technique. Generally speaking, the next forecast's value (F_t) is equal to the sum of the previous forecast's value (F_{t-1}) and the product of the forecasting error ($A_{t1} - F_{t-1}$), where the actual and previous forecasts are subtracted from one another, and the smoothing constant (a), which is equal to a percentage of the forecasting error. To make this more concrete, Stevenson (2015) provided the following formula:

$$F_t = F_{t-1} + \propto \left(A_{t-1} - F_{t-1} \right).$$

This formula readily lends itself to straightforward implementation. To illustrate, let's use information from Table 5.1. Assume that the goal is to estimate the school year's enrollment values and that thus far we have employed a three-school year moving average technique to do so. Since we have already calculated the moving average using the last three periods of data, which is often recommended (Stevenson, 2015), we can now quickly calculate the forecasted enrollments for school year 2012–2013 using exponential smoothing.

First, assume that the forecasted value of 23,533.3[3] for school year 2011–2012 was off by 500 students and the actual value equals 23,033.3. Second, assume that the smoothing constant (a) is .15. With this information, the next step is to correctly specify the values for each part of the equation. The equation for this example should look like this:

$$F_{12} = 23,533.3 + .15(23,033.3 - 23,533.3) = 23,458.3.$$

This estimate directly accounts for the error between forecasted and actual values when projecting the next school year's enrollment forecast. If one wishes to use exponential smoothing for the next school year (2013–2014), then the method is the same. To demonstrate, assume that the actual demand for school year 2012–2013 is off by 250 students so that the actual number is 23,208.3. Then the equation for period 13 takes the following form:

$$F_{13} = 23,458.3 + .15(23,208.3 - 23,458.3) = 23,420.8.$$

Based upon the assumptions regarding the smoothing constant, the budget manager can continue to project future values in this way.

While a more powerful and sophisticated tool than averaging methods, there are some important limitations when employing this technique. Much like the weighted moving average presented earlier, exponential smoothing requires rather subjective decisions regarding the smoothing constant. In most instances, the smoothing constant takes on a value of between .05 and .50 where lower values assume stability in the underlying averages and higher numbers imply a lack of stability (Stevenson, 2015).

Additionally, the forecasted values become more reactive as the value of the smoothing constant increases from zero to one. This means that the P-12 budget manager should have a valid and clear rationale for the choice of a smoothing constant level even when using software that can automatically change a values when errors become too large.

Correlation Analysis

Before moving to the more sophisticated analysis of two variables, it is important to highlight a relatively easy and extremely useful measure for forecasting relationships-correlation analysis. While the previous section has provided a clear approach for forecasting using averages, this technique is focused more upon the movement of variables in relation to one another. The usefulness of correlation analysis instead of, or with, regression analysis is that it provides a readily accessible measure of the magnitude of relationship between two variables. Say, for example, that we wish to examine the relationship between total enrollment and students qualifying for special education services and the total program for the school district.

The measure of correlation (Pearson r) can tell us how strong this relationship is and can easily be carried out for a number of variables simultaneously with Excel or other statistical software packages. The general equation[4] for computing this relationship is as follows (Stevenson, 2015):

$$r = \frac{n\left(\sum xy\right) - \left(\sum x\right)\left(\sum y\right)}{\sqrt{n\left(\sum x^2\right) - \left(\sum x\right)^2}\sqrt{n\left(\sum y^2\right) - \left(\sum y\right)^2}}.$$

As the measure is bounded between −1 and +1, it can tell us both the direction and the strength of the relationship. For the most part, relationships ranging from .70 to .80 and above are considered strong, between .30 and .70 moderate, and below .30 weak (Stevenson, 2015; Trochim & Donnelly, 2007). Additionally, the sign indicates the direction of the relationship. So, for example, let's say that local revenue from property taxes and state support share a −.85 relationship. This would suggest that revenues from local property taxes and state support move in a strong and opposite direction from one another.

If the negative sign were left off, then it would be clear that the two would share a strong positive relationship indicating that they move in a similar direction (if one moves up the other tends to as well and vice versa). When used appropriately, P-12 budget managers can forecast expected relationships and their magnitude. When coupled with regression analysis, this makes for an especially powerful prediction tool. What is more, many statistical software packages and Excel include a canned option for determining if the relationship is statistically significant.[5]

Finally, when used with regression analysis, the square of the correlation coefficient (r) provides an easily understandable measure for estimating how much of the variance in the dependent variable is explained by the independent variable or variables (if used with multiple regression). The interpretation of the r^2 coefficient is similar to that of the r-coefficient earlier. However, in this instance, the r^2 statistic informs us how well the independent variable (x) accounts for the variance in the dependent variable (y).

Another caveat is that this goodness-of-fit statistic is always positive given that it is the square of the correlation coefficient. Readers should note that the

r^2 statistic is only one of a variety of goodness-of-fit measures. For example, a typical goodness-of-fit measure for categorical data is a chi-square (χ^2) statistic. Hence, it is imperative that the budget manager understand the data and how best to use different forecasting techniques and tools for making appropriate budget projections.

Using Linear Models and Regression for Forecasting

Linear models and regression analysis provide a good predictive approach to forecasting based on linear trends rather than averages. In its most basic form, a linear model is expressed as:

$$Y_t = a + b(x).$$

Where Y_t is equal to the forecasted value in time t; a is equal to the intercept that is the value that Y_t would take on if x equals zero; b is equal to the slope of the line of best fit; and x is the independent variable. Essentially, this model is telling us that Y (the forecasted value for time t) will be equal to the sum of the baseline intercept (a) and x multiplied by b. For many individuals who have not had statistics in some time, or who are unfamiliar with this equation at all, b in the equation is simply telling us how Y_t changes when x changes.

Based on the purposes of this chapter, x will be equal to the time period t. So, the equation looks exactly the same as before with t standing in for x (Stevenson, 2015). This formula allows us to calculate trend values when it is assumed that the relationship between x and y are linear. This model expresses the relationship between x and y formally, and also makes assumptions about the relationship between the two variables (Dunn, 2012).

Regression Forecasting

Before moving into the specific mechanics of regression forecasting, we should underscore the important distinctions regarding correlational and causal analysis. Many individuals who employ regression techniques for forecasting are often unaware of these distinctions. Because each type of analysis introduces certain assumptions, only fundamental differences are explored.

First, and in most instances, P-12 budget managers will carry out correlational forecasting. This means that the relationships examined and explained using regression analysis should be understood in terms of their association, not causes. That is, interpretation of the estimates of the relationship between x and y should be expressed as associations (they move in relation to one another in a particular manner; for example, as enrollment increases in a school district expenses increase as well) and not that x causes y. If one wishes to make causal claims, there are techniques for doing so. Causal analysis makes claims regarding the impact of *x* on *y* in terms of cause and effect; *x* causes *y* and *x* is not simply associated with *y*.

While this is an important distinction, it is outside the scope of the current text to explore causal analysis as a topic because it requires much more sophisticated estimation techniques.[6] Additionally, it is possible to employ multiple regression when more than one explanatory variable (*x*) is used for forecasting. This technique allows for the inclusion of many known drivers of specific outcome variable (*y*). For those interested in a detailed treatment of these two subjects, we suggest referencing Box & Jenkins (2008) and Stevenson (2015).

Returning to linear regression, the most typical modeling choice used by P-12 budget managers is ordinary least squares (OLS). OLS seeks to find a straight line that minimizes the distance of the historical data points from this line of best fit. For example, in Figure 5.1, all 10 data points for the number of students are plotted (squares) and a line (linear trend) is fitted.

A much touted benefit of using regression analysis in forecasting is that its assumptions are clear, and it is relatively easy to implement using excel or statistical packages such as SPSS, STATA, or SAS. Additionally, the linear trend line calculated using OLS is as close as possible to the historical data points. As noted by Finker et al. (2013), not only is it unlikely that all historical points would fall along a straight line, but any other line would be further away as well. This means that the closeness of the line to historical data points will result in future, estimated points, closer to the actual future values. This concept is illustrated in the data presented in Figure 5.2 and Table 5.2.

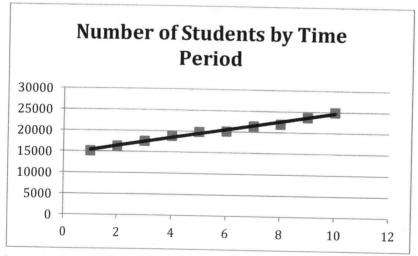

Figure 5.1   Example of Data Points Plotted with Linear Trend Line Superimposed.
Source: Authors.

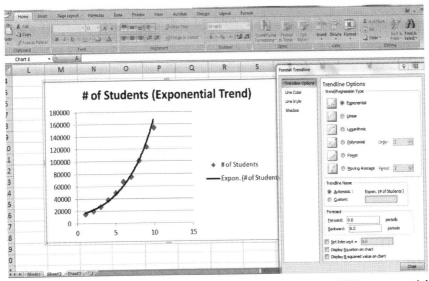

Figure 5.2 Screenshot of Trendline Options in Microsoft Excel Using an Exponential Trend. *Source*: Authors.

Let's look at an example using our fictional dataset from before.
First, we should plot the data to determine whether or not a linear trend is evident. From Figure 5.1, we can see that it is. Now recall the formula:

$$Y_t = a + b(t).$$

In order to employ this formula to forecast correctly, we must find the values of a and b that will provide us with a linear trend based on the assumptions

Table 5.2 Fictional Data Set for Forecasting Student Enrollments Using Linear Regression (OLS)

School Year (t)	Number of Students (Y)	School Year* Number of Students (t*y)	Time Squared (t²)
2001–2002	15,123	15,123	1
2002–2003	16,345	32,690	4
2003–2004	17,567	52,701	9
2004–2005	18,789	75,156	16
2005–2006	19,901	99,505	25
2006–2007	20,123	120,738	36
2007–2008	21,456	150,192	49
2008–2009	22,000	176,000	64
2009–2010	23,678	213,102	81
2010–2011	24,922	249,220	100
$\Sigma t = 55$	$\Sigma y = 199{,}904$	$\Sigma ty = 1{,}184{,}427$	$t^2 = 385$

of OLS. To do so, we need two more equations. To calculate our *b* value, we will need to use the formula that follows. Following Stevenson (2015, p. 93), this is expressed formally as:

$$b = \frac{n\sum tY - \sum t \sum y}{n\sum (t^2) - \left(\sum t\right)^2}.$$

Therefore, the value should be:

$$b = \frac{10(1,184,427) - 55(199,904)}{10(385) - 55(55)} \text{ or } 1,029.76.$$

Readers should notice that the value of ΣtY (1,184,427) is different from the value of ΣtΣy (10,994,720); this matters computationally for the estimating equation.

For our next variable the formal expression is:

$$a = \frac{\sum Y - b\sum t}{n}$$

Therefore, the values should be:

$$a = \frac{199,904 - 1,029.76(55)}{10} \text{ or } 14,326.72.$$

Based on this information, the linear trend line is equal to:

$$Y_t = 14,326.72 + 1,029.76(t).$$

Therefore, if we wish to estimate what the forecasted number of students will be based on OLS estimates, we simply plug that number in for *t*. In this case, we would expect that student numbers would be equal to 25,654.08 (14,326.72 + 1,029.76(11)). Now suppose we wish to do the same thing for period 13. We simply employ the same technique and come up with 27,713.60 (14,326.72 + 1,029.76(13)). As is evident, the linear models employed here return much higher forecasts on student numbers than any of the averaging techniques. This short illustration should serve as a good example of the ways in which the underlying structure and specific approaches impact the resulting forecast.

While regression analysis is a powerful tool for forecasting, some limitations remain. First, we must make sure that the relationship being modeled is logical. If not, estimates will not be valid. Next, just like any other forecasting technique, the assumptions about the data can limit the usefulness of the results. If inappropriate assumptions have been made, the analysis is for naught. Another consideration is that simple regression analysis is appropriate only for the case where there is one dependent (*Y*) variable and one independent (*X*) variable. If not, then other techniques that include multivariate regression should be considered.

Also, the data requirements for regression analysis tend to be rather large with the minimum number of observations being 20–30 for valid forecasting (Stevenson, 2015). Finally, the linear technique presented here makes a very strong statement about the relationship of the variables. If the data do not share a linear relationship, the use of this technique is not correct (Finkler et al., 2013). Techniques for dealing with this situation are presented in the next section on curvilinear models.

CURVILINEAR MODELS: A BRIEF OVERVIEW

In the previous section we highlighted the benefits and limitations of regression analysis and linear assumptions. While we indicate that regression analysis is a powerful tool in the forecaster's arsenal, a major limitation remains. Namely, the linear approach is based on the assumption that the relationships under examination follow a straight line as illustrated in Figure 5.1 (Finkler, et al., 2013). When relationships among variables do not exist in this manner, there are ways to either deal with the curvilinear nature of the relationship or employ mathematical transformations of the data to make it more linear.

Typically, forecasters will encounter four types of curvilinear trends in a set of data: exponential, logarithmic, polynomial, and power. While we treat moving averages as its own approach in this chapter, it should be understood that moving averages can also have curvilinear traits and, therefore, data should be plotted, if possible, before imposing a trend line upon it.

First is exponential transformation of the data. What this does is to transform the data into an exponential function that can show underlying trends based on a value changing at an increasingly upward or downward manner. Next is the logarithmic transformation approach. This transformation method is especially good for data that exhibit rapid changes that smooth out over time or that clearly show growth or decline that is persistent. This is an approach often used to help smooth data fluctuations that, if graphed or examined in their raw state, would make interpretation difficult.

Another approach is the polynomial (cyclical) method, which is especially useful for data that vary in a cyclical fashion (up and down) over time. The reason for such variability is often due to timing, seasonality, or economic cycles. Finally, power trends are useful for data that display a relationship where the values of the data are increasing at a specific rate at regular points over time. A limitation of this approach, however, is that because it employs a power equation, it cannot deal with values that are either zero or negative (Dunn, 2012; Finkler et al., 2013; Stevenson, 2015).

The great thing about using any type of trend line is that there exist many software packages that either specialize in this or provide tools for carrying out a trend analysis. For example, Excel provides a great and readily accessible means for plotting data and examining trends. The available trend line options are illustrated in Figure 5.2.[7]

JUDGMENT IN FORECASTING

For much of this chapter the focus has been upon rather mechanistic methods for forecasting future states of events. In this section, we turn to what is arguably the most important component of good forecasting—human judgment. As noted throughout this chapter, the assumptions made about the data, relationships, and local variables, which are all based on human judgment, underpin the relevance and utility of forecasts. To help explain this role more carefully, we will consider the role of multiple factors that impact the forecasting process in turn.

The P-12 budget manager plays a direct role in the forecasting of future events/values that matter to decision-making. In many cases, it is the P-12 budget manager's role to determine the assumptions that should be included in the model. In some cases, the P-12 budget manager chooses the approach. In any event, the budget manager can have a great deal of influence over forecasts as well as their validity when choices are based upon the information available. For example, a fluctuation in an external variable may be of great consequence to one individual when conducting a forecast and of little importance to another.

Another important and related consideration is the role of budget philosophy. As highlighted in chapter 2, because educational organizations tend to have processes in place for allocating resources, knowing how this might impact the forecasting approach and assumptions is very important. Regardless of the type of approach employed locally, most P-12 budget managers develop a forecasting style that mirrors their philosophy of budget management. However, even the best educational leaders should take care not to remain too committed to a budgeting philosophy that may or may not reflect the current and anticipated circumstances facing the organization. Instead, historical data, sound analysis, and scanning of the external environment for possible instability can contribute to an optimal forecasting strategy.

In the end, each of the forecasting strategies discussed in this chapter represents an educated guess on future trends based on the best data available.

The word that must be stressed in that sentence is that forecasting is a scientific manner of *guessing*. For this reason, a wise P-12 budget manager will diligently determine the optimal forecasting strategy for a particular school district.

How? As was stated earlier, the best practice is to use historical data to gauge the accuracy of different forecasting strategies. For example, if you are entering the 2020–2021 school year and are interested in altering the weights used in the forecasting formula, then you would be well served to use the forecasting formula with the new weights on historical data—such as the data from the 2015–2016 school year. Assuming you were interested in forecasting student enrollment figures, you could run the formula based on the data available in June and then compare the findings to the actual enrollment figures reported to the state during the October 1 student count. Some guiding questions around such a practice could include: How accurate was the forecasting formula? Could it be altered to be more accurate? Did it over- or underestimate?

The practice of testing forecasting formulas is a sound practice that should be employed by P-12 budget managers regularly, not just when the forecasting formula is being altered. It is imperative to remember that the extraneous variables, or the factors beyond the control of school district officials, are constantly in flux and a forecasting formula that works today may be less effective the following school year. In short, the P-12 budget manager involved in forecasting should only assume that the current forecasting strategy is somewhat flawed and can be improved.

Finally, the role of expert judgment should not be understated. In fact, in many cases, it is expertise that allows budget managers and analysts to anticipate events that might be just beyond the horizon. While there are some formal techniques for judgmental forecasting, such as the Delphi Technique, Consumer Surveys, Cross-Impact Analysis, and Feasibility Assessment (Dunn, 2012; Stevenson, 2015), incorporating expertise into forecasting processes suggests that those involved in the process recognize it as both science and art (Finkler et al., 2013).

Last, expertise confronts one of the primary limitations to regression and other types of mathematical forecasting. Because the mathematical techniques presented earlier assume that the past is a good indicator of the future, the techniques and formulas are not fruitful when sharp discontinuities arise. Effective P-12 budget managers must strive to develop an expertise related to internal and external environments that could positively or negatively impact the accuracy of future forecasting. This expertise to accurately forecast in a way that controls for internal and external environments is often underrated in public education.

CONCLUSION

In this chapter we have covered the basic tools and techniques available to budget managers and analysts when anticipating a future state of events or for examining the consequences of possible courses of action. We have highlighted the fact that although forecasting is often seen as a technical or procedural exercise, it usefulness lies in the ability to access good data and skills. It also relies heavily upon the judgment and assumptions of the individuals working within a specific context. Because the organizational conditions of schools, colleges, and universities can often be idiosyncratic, knowing the local culture, context, and conditions makes forecasts that much more reliable.

Finally, it is always important to remember that though many approaches to forecasting take on formal logical structures that are mathematical in nature, the ability of the forecast to provide useful information is primarily dependent upon the assumptions made about the model and the human judgment that goes into interpreting the results. Regardless of the method employed, there will always be a difference between the true values and the forecasted ones. The job of those responsible with forecasting is to get as close as possible.

GUIDING QUESTIONS

The following questions address many of the key concepts covered in chapter 5. Readers should be able to answer these questions upon completing the chapter:

1. Why do public administrators overseeing budgets carry out forecasting? What is the use?
2. Why are forecasts always off by some amount? Is this a big problem? Why or why not?
3. How should P-12 budget managers deal with significant but unforeseen events when forecasting?
4. How does human judgment come into play in forecasting? How is this related to budget philosophy?

ADDITIONAL READING

Those students desiring additional information on the concepts addressed in chapter 5 should consult the following:

Baker, B. D. 2001. Can flexible non-linear modeling tell us anything new about educational productivity? *Economics of Education Review*, 20(1), 81–92. doi: 10.1016/S0272-7757(99)00051-5.

Baker, B. D., & C. E. Richards. 1999. A comparison of conventional linear regression methods and neural networks for forecasting educational spending. *Economics of Education Review*, 18(4), 405–15. doi: 10.1016/S0272-7757(99)00003-5.

Tang, H. V., & M. Yin. 2012. Forecasting performance of grey prediction for education expenditure and school enrollment. *Economics of Education Review*, 31(4), 452–62. doi: 10.1016/j.econedurev.2011.12.007.

EXERCISES

Fictional Dataset

1. Using the fictional dataset here, and Microsoft Excel if available, forecast and compare the following for both enrollment figures and per pupil expenditures:
   a. 3-year moving average
   b. 5-year moving average
   c. 3-year weighted moving average

School Year	Enrollment Figures	Per Pupil Expenditure (State and Local Dollars)	3-Year Weights	5-Year Weights
1	1492.31	2131.23		
2	1898.91	2932.32		
3	2129.75	3170.64		
4	2405.39	4210.94		
5	2438.37	4414.92		
6	2747.66	4665.64		
7	3656.07	4885.36		
8	3996.81	4966.73		
9	4039.79	5268.67		
10	4166.03	5330.20		
11	4468.68	5804.23		
12	5195.66	5804.29		
13	5720.69	6591.48		
14	6034.75	6691.75		
15	6087.02	6921.12		
16	6303.96	7383.40		0.10
17	6310.82	7960.05		0.15
18	7679.58	7979.40	0.15	0.20
19	7811.71	7994.73	0.35	0.25
20	8329.63	8279.02	0.50	0.30
		Total Weight	**1.0**	**1.0**

d. 5-year weighted moving average

e. 3-year exponential smoothing with a smoothing constant (*a*) of .20 and a difference in actual versus forecasted values for time period 20 of $300.

Finally, explain briefly why moving average, weighted average, and exponential smoothing forecasts differ.

2. Using Microsoft Excel and the dataset here, answer the following for both enrollment figures and per pupil expenditures:

a. How closely correlated are these two variables related over the entire dataset based on the (Pearson) correlation coefficient?

b. What is the direction of the (Pearson) correlation coefficient's sign? What does this indicate with regard to the relationship? How would this change if the sign were in the opposite direction?

c. Predict a 3-year forecast using the example provided in this chapter.

d. Complete the same exercise as earlier, but this time use the regression function in Excel.

e. What are some of the limitations of using regression forecasting? How does this relate to curvilinear models?

3. What is the cost of a poor hire? To answer this, you need to determine the following:

a. What is the salary of a new teacher (no graduate degree) in the school district where you work?

b. In addition to salary, how much money is allocated to the annual benefits (retirement, health insurance, dental insurance, life insurance, etc.) of a new hire?

c. Imagine that after a year, you, as the principal, nonrenew the teacher and that person is unable to find another teaching position. In the fall, the person applies for unemployment benefits. How much money will the school district have to dedicate to unemployment benefits?

d. What is the cost of a poor hire financially? Add up your answers to a, b, and c.

e. What will you do to mitigate the likelihood of making a bad hire?

NOTES

1. Although not referred to as such, these three qualities are derived from Terenzini's (1999) three tiers of organizational intelligence.

2. The "moving" part in this equation has to do with the fact that the average moves to the next group of periods, be they three, five, or more. Hence, the average moves to the next group of included periods.

3. It is unlikely that the institution will have 0.3 FTEs; however, for illustrative purposes, we include exact values. In some cases these values would require rounding for appropriate interpretation.

4. In using this example, the authors are cognizant of the fact that we present only the most typical correlation coefficient measure, Pearson's *r*. Students who are working with discrete data, or, for example, survey data, should take care to use the correct correlation measure such as Spearman's Rho, Cramer's V, or Point-Biserial.

5. It is typical to examine the relationships' statistical significance at the 0.05 level but can also be as high as 0.10.

6. A good introductory text, titled *Methods Matter*, is provided by Murnane & Willet (2011).

7. To get to this point, one need simply insert a scatter-plot graph of the data. Once this is done, simply right click on any of the data points in the graph and choose "Add Trendline." Once this option is chosen, a screen similar to that shown in Figure 5.2 will open and you can explore the many options that exist for trending the data.

Phase II

DEVELOPING AND OVERSEEING THE TOTAL PROGRAM

With the foundational knowledge discussed in phase I, the aspiring P-12 budget manager is now prepared to explore concepts related to developing and overseeing the school district's total program and the school's operating budget. Specifically, the discussion related to phase II will include a review of the typical budget cycle for school districts. In addition, the concepts of budget oversight, auditing budgets, and variance analysis are presented. These concepts, in conjunction with the foundational material covered in phase I, will empower aspiring P-12 budget managers with the expertise necessary to effectively and efficiently manage a budget in a way that maximizes the educational opportunities of all students within the organization.

Chapter 6

The Budget Cycle

Managing budgets is relentless work. There are previous budgets to close as well as current budgets to oversee and, as if that was not enough, future budgets requiring development and adoption. Effective P-12 budget managers understand and utilize the budget cycle to help them in the development and adoption of future budgets for public education. What is the budget cycle? The budget cycle encompasses the steps taken to create a budget, or the process of developing a budget up to the point when the governing board approves the budget.

Given that P-12 budgets rely on public funds generated through the levying of taxes, those entrusted with managing budgets for school districts and schools are familiar with the volatility between budgets from one year to the next. As a result of this volatility, P-12 budget managers should become familiar with the budget cycle to ensure that all future budgets capture anticipated economic trends and align with the school district's vision, mission, and goals.

The content included in this chapter is designed to provide students of the P-12 budgetary process a foundational understanding of the budget cycle. In addition, the material included in this chapter will discuss the different strategies related to building a P-12 budget during times of economic growth, or when the school district's budget is expanding, and budgeting during periods of economic reduction, or when the school district's total program is shrinking due to external factors. Finally, the chapter concludes with a number of exercises designed to provide students of the budget cycle opportunities to apply the theoretical concepts discussed in the chapter to real situations.

BUDGETING IN PERIODS OF ECONOMIC GROWTH

Why would a public organization's budget grow? In the world of P-12 education, there are four possible reasons:

1. An increase to the state's budget—During periods of economic growth states collect more funds from taxpayers than was anticipated. These funds can either be returned to the taxpayers, if deemed excess, or used to increase existing state budgets. If state policymakers employ the latter option, then school districts would receive additional funds from the state for either the current or future total program.
2. An increase to the local net assessed value (NAV)—Local property tax revenues are based on the NAV of all the properties within a school district's boundaries. If there is an increase to the school district's NAV, then the value of each mill increases. As the value of a mill increases so does the total money generated through property taxes, and these funds are added to the school district's existing budget. It should be noted here that the process of reassessing the value of properties typically happens on a multiyear cycle (two-year, three-year, or even four-year cycle).
3. An increase in student enrollment—School districts can also experience economic growth at a micro-level if the student population is growing. For example, if school district leaders create a budget based on an anticipated student enrollment of 1,000 students and then, after the actual student count data are tallied, realize they are serving 1,050 students, the school district's budget increased by 5%, or $500,000 (assuming the per pupil expenditure was $10,000). However, there will also be increased expenses associated with serving these additional 50 students (hiring a new teacher or two, paraprofessional support, etc.), and so not all of the $500,000 represents an increase to the school district's total program.
4. A voter-approved mill levy override—If, in November, voters in a school district approve a proposed mill levy override, then, starting in January, the school district's budget receives the total funding of the voter-approved mill levy override. Depending upon the particulars of the voter-approved mill levy override, the school district will continue to receive the approved amount of money annually for the duration of the mill. Unless the mill has a sunset, or a time when the mill will expire, the school district's total program is guaranteed the annual increase indefinitely.

Specific Points to Consider When Creating a P-12 Budget during Periods of Economic Growth

There are a number of strategies related to the creation of a budget during periods of economic growth. The first priority should be to restore cuts to services or programs if the period of economic growth comes on the heels of economic and budgetary cuts. During economic downturns, school district officials will typically eliminate or reduce nonessential programs to "weather the storm." If cuts have occurred in the past, then the first item to discuss should be the need to restore the previously cut services or programs.

The next discussion point should center on the school district's vision statement, mission statement, and goals. School district officials should explore strategies for better achieving the school district's stated purposes in these documents. For example, if a school district's mission statement stresses the fact that all students can learn and data show that too many students are leaving the third grade reading below grade level, then the decision may be to allocate more of the "new" funds to early literacy programs and services.

Next, school district officials should consider the needs of its workforce. Public education is a personnel heavy industry, and most people who go into this amazing profession do so with the realization that they are not going to make as much money as they might in other professions. However, this is not to say that those in education do not value increases to their salary or benefits. School district officials, school board members, and state policymakers must realize that a happy workforce is always preferable to an unhappy one, and the easiest way to create a happy workforce is through pay increases during times when a school district has surplus money in its total program.

Finally, those entrusted with deciding where to allocate additional funds during periods of economic growth must be cognizant of one-time and ongoing expenses. One-time expenses, such as an investment aimed at infusing technology into every classroom, are easier to budget for during periods of economic growth than ongoing expenses, such as an increase in salaries. Given that budget managers are encouraged to be fiscally conservative, it seems logical to assume that, even during periods of economic growth, the next year will bring a significant dip in anticipated revenues. With such an assumption, one-time expenses are preferable to ongoing expenses.

BUDGETING IN PERIODS OF ECONOMIC REDUCTION

The reasons for periods of economic reduction are going to be opposite of those discussed in the previous section (periods of economic growth). Specifically, for P-12, factors that contribute to the reduction in a school district's budget include:

1. A decrease to the state's budget—If state officials build a budget around an anticipated tax revenue base and, due to an economic down turn or a recession, the taxes fail to generate the anticipated revenue, then school district budgets are going to receive cuts (especially given the fact that in

most states, P-12 funding accounts for 30–40% of the state's total budget). Both the state and the local school district will have contingency funds to help account for a periodic dip in anticipated revenues, but if the period of economic reduction lasts multiple years, then state policymakers will cut funding to school districts.

2. A decrease to the local NAV—Historically, property taxes represent a stable revenue source for local government. However, property values are not impervious to economic swings and can fluctuate enough to negatively impact a school district's total program. If there is a downturn in a school district's NAV, then the value of each mill decreases.

3. A decrease in student enrollment—School districts with declining enrollment also face shrinking budgets since a school district's total program, or annual budget, is based on the number of students being educated in the school district. The funding formulas in some states mitigate the negative impact of declining enrollment by allowing school districts to report the current student count or a three-year (or five-year) average, whichever is greater. The impact of averages on the revenues for a school district is illustrated in Table 6.1.

The use of averages provides the school district illustrated in Table 6.1 with higher student enrollment figures than it would have if the state used only the actual enrollment figures each year. Averages are most beneficial to smaller school districts due to the fiscal impact a slight decrease in student enrollment can have on their total program.

Specific Strategies to Consider When Creating a P-12 Budget during Periods of Economic Reduction

The natural tendency for educators is to insulate students from the negative impact of budgetary cuts. Although this approach makes perfect sense, after all educators entered this profession to help young people reach their full potential, it can actually have a negative impact on public education. Ultimately, parents are the best advocates for public education. If, during periods of economic reductions, parents are not made aware of the impact

Table 6.1 Average Student Enrollment

School Year	Actual Enrollment	Average Enrollment
2009–2010	1,532	–
2010–2011	1,473	1,503
2011–2012	1,488	1,497
2012–2013	1,443	1,484
2013–2014	1,457	1,479

that cutting a budget has on the educational experiences of their children, then public education is losing a powerful voice that can influence policymakers.

An example of this point can offer better insight. Prior to approaching local voters with a bond proposal to build a new high school, the school district's chief financial officer needed to purchase portable classrooms. Instead of purchasing the nicest available portables, this leader opted for some extremely dilapidated temporary classrooms and ended up placing them in the most prominent position at the high school. Parents saw what the school district was using as temporary space, realized the legitimate need, and passed the bond initiative in November.

With that said, if the budget reduction is anticipated to be a one-time event, then school district leaders should look at budget items that will have the least impact on student achievement. Examples of cuts to budgets that could be made one time to weather a fiscal storm include: doing away with professional development for one year (especially if the school district also has instructional coaches in place), delaying technology upgrades for a year, or slight increases to class sizes. This final option would allow school district leaders to reduce the total number of educators in the school district through attrition, as opposed to a reduction in force.

Educational leaders overseeing budgets should have clearly defined answers to the following questions prior to having to reduce a budget:

- What principles guide your decision-making process when cutting a budget?
- What would you not cut from a school or school district budget under any circumstance? Why?
- What would you be willing to cut from a budget? Why?

Then, when required to cut a budget, educational leaders will have already established their guiding principles and will be better positioned to follow those principles. Ideally, decisions around reducing a budget should be made in collaboration with other leaders within the organization to ensure that all decisions are genuinely best for students and represent the interests of all within the organization.

THE P-12 BUDGET CYCLE

The budget cycle for P-12 public education is best explained as a sequential process. The overall steps include planning and projections, presentation and adoption, and management. Each of the steps in a budget cycle are explained in Table 6.2. The budget cycle for P-12 public education contains quite a few

Table 6.2 The P-12 Budget Cycle, Fiscal Year 2013–2014

Overall Step	Task	Timeline	Description
Planning and projection	Program review	Fall 2012	School and school district officials assess current program expenditures and the benefits associated with each cost, or the return on each investment. Certain programs could be deemed inefficient and discontinued if the cost of the program exceeds the benefit to the school or the school district. If officials decide to discontinue a particular program, the change will not take effect until the following school year.
	Enrollment projections	Fall through Spring 2012–2013	Student enrollment figures represent the primary revenue sources for school districts and schools. As a result, school district and school officials work to accurately anticipate future enrollment data by examining birth rates, actual enrollment figures, construction trends, and student attrition or retention data.
	Expenditure projections	Spring 2013	Another step in collecting all of the necessary data to develop a preliminary budget is for school district and school leaders to identify expenditure projections for the upcoming fiscal year. This could include adjustments to employee wages and benefits, materials, fuel expenses, etc.
Presentation and adoption	School board workshops	Spring 2013	With all of the projections related to revenues (enrollments), program reviews, and expenditures completed, school district leaders begin to work with the school board members on the development of a draft budget. Most of this work is completed in workshop meetings. Workshops are held for the purpose of educating school board members on the budgetary process, discussing the projected fiscal solvency of the school district, and deciding upon the direction of the school district for the upcoming school year.
	Preliminary budget development	Spring 2013	With the input from the school board, school district officials take the data collected in the planning and projection stage to develop a preliminary budget for the school district.
	Review and revise the preliminary budget	Spring 2013	The preliminary budget for the school district is now shared with all stakeholders (school administrators, teacher association leaders, parents, etc.) to seek additional input. Any input provided by stakeholders can result in revisions to the preliminary budget to better capture the desires of all stakeholders.

Presentation and adoption	Present the final budget to the school board	May 2013	Typically by May—roughly two months before the new budget goes into effect—school district officials present the final version of the budget to the school board. The school board can approve the budget as it stands, solicit additional information, or require revisions.
	Adoption of the final budget	June 2013	Once the school board is comfortable with the proposed school district budget, there is a vote held to formally adopt new budget. The approved budget formally goes into effect on July 1, 2013.
Management	Meet with county assessors	August 2013	The superintendent or designee will meet with the county assessors in states where property tax is levied to fund a portion of public education to certify the net assessed value (NAV) of the properties within the school district.
	Report homeless count	September 2013	School district officials have to report to the state the total number of homeless students attending since these students receive additional funding from the federal government.
	Actual enrollment data	October 2013	Realizing that the entire school district budget is based on projected student enrollment figures (generated months prior to the start of the fiscal year), school district officials need to determine and report actual enrollment data to the state by early October.
	Mill levy certification	December 2013	School district officials certify to county commissioners and the state department of education the mill levies required for the local contribution to the school district's total program (or annual budget) in states that use property tax to fund a portion of public education.
	Military pupil count	January 2014	In states where school districts receive additional funding for children of military personnel, a formal count of these students must occur and be reported to the state by the middle of January.
	Independent or external auditor	November 2013	All school districts are required to have an independent or external auditor review the previous fiscal year's budget and transactions to ensure that all fiscal interactions were completed in accordance with state and federal guidelines.
	Overseeing the budget	Ongoing	On a regular basis, school district officials and school officials oversee the entire budget to ensure individual accounts are not being mismanaged.
	Audit report to the state	December 2014	Finally, to close out the 2013–2014 fiscal year, school district leaders are required to submit the report from the independent or external auditor to the state.

steps and may appear a bit cumbersome. However, each of these steps exist to ensure that limited public dollars are spent effectively and efficiently to, ultimately, promote student learning.

CONCLUSION

An understanding of the budget cycle is essential for educational leaders and aspiring educational leaders to be able to develop, manage, and oversee existing budgets. The information covered in this chapter illustrates that the budget cycle, like laundry at home, never goes away—a P-12 budget manager is never finished with the budget cycle. The reason for this statement is that at any given time, a P-12 budget manager is doing some combination of the following activities: closing out a previous budget, managing a current budget, and preparing for a future budget.

GUIDING QUESTIONS

The following questions address many of the key concepts covered in chapter 6. Readers should be able to answer these questions upon completing the chapter:

1. What factors would contribute to the growth of a school district budget? Why?
2. What are the different points to consider when managing a budget during a period of growth as opposed to a period of declining budget in public education?
3. What is the role of both internal and external oversight when it comes to managing a public school budget?
4. As you consider the budget cycle, what are some challenges that budget managers face as they develop budgets for the upcoming school year?

ADDITIONAL READING

Those readers desiring additional information on the concepts addressed in chapter 6 should consult the following:

Garner, W. C. 2004. *Education finance for school leaders: Strategic planning and administration.* Upper Saddle River, NJ: Pearson. (Pay particular attention to chapter 9.)

Thompson, D. C., R. C. Wood, & F. E. Crampton. 2008. *Money & schools* (4th ed.). Larchmont, NY: Eye on Education. (Pay particular attention to chapter 5.)

EXERCISES

Using the data in Table 6.3, complete the two exercises.

1. You just got a call from the superintendent, and she asks you (as the principal of the school) to cut 10% from your budget ($466,000). Go through and make the necessary cuts, and pay attention to the guiding principles you use to make the cuts.
2. You just got a call from the superintendent, and she tells you (as the principal of the school) that due to unanticipated revenue sources from the state,

Table 6.3 Fictional Elementary School Budget: School Finance Elementary School (SFES)

School Configuration		School Budget		
Element	SFES	Category	Number	Total Cost ($)
Grades	K–5	Core teachers	30.5	2,043,500
Enrollment	600	SpEd teachers	6	402,000
Class size	K–3:18	Instructional coaches	2.5	167,500
	4–5:25			
Full-day kindergarten	Yes	Tutors	3	201,000
% Disabled	10% (60 students)	ELL teacher	0.5	33,500
% Free Lunch	54% (324 students)	Ext. day	2.5	167,500
ELL	8% (48 students)	Summer school	2.5	167,500
		SpEd support	4	268,000
School Personnel		Gifted		14,440
Core teachers	K–3:22.5	Substitutes		67,905
	4–5:8			
SpEd teachers	6	Pupil support	3.15	211,050
Inst. coach	2.5	Aides	2.5	53,200
Tutors	3	Media center	1.33	89,110
ELL teacher	.5	Principal	1.33	133,000
Extended day	2.5	Secretary	1.0	38,000
Summer school	2.5	Clerical	1.33	50,540
		PD		60,600
		Technology		150,000
Gifted teacher	$14,440	Inst. materials		85,000
Substitutes	$67,905	Student activities		115,200
Pupil support	3.15	Custodian	3	115,000
Aides	2.66	Custodial sup		15,000
Media center	1.33	Office sup		15,000
Principal	1.33			
Secretary	1.0	Total		4,663,505
Clerical	1.33			

you have an additional $400,000 to apply to the existing budget (use the original data reported in Table 6.3—not the adjusted data after you made the cuts in exercise 1). Add the money to the budget and be cognizant of the guiding principles you use as you incorporate these additional funds into the budget.

3. As you go through these two exercises, which are artificial, what additional information would you have appreciated to be able to make a more informed decision?

Chapter 7

Oversight and Budget
Variance Analysis

An important part of examination and oversight of a school district or school performance is to analyze the variance between forecasted and actual numbers. While we note in chapter 3 that a small variance is likely, large variances could indicate some trouble with the analytic approach, data, or assumptions. In this chapter, we outline techniques that allow the P-12 budget manager to examine variances and provide some guidance for dealing with them to improve oversight. Based on the rather cyclical nature of revenue and expenditure patterns, knowing when and where (in which part of the budget) to expect variances will help P-12 budget managers provide useful information to those charged with budget oversight. Additionally, we briefly examine the role that accounting standards play in understanding budget variances and how this can impact the decision-making process as well as the role of auditing in budget oversight.

VARIANCES IN REVENUES AND EXPENDITURES

For budget oversight to be effective, it must systematically examine whether forecasts are within a reasonable range when compared to observed revenues and expenditures. A first step to this process is to examine the budget in parts. While the budget itself and budgeting are often treated as a single document or process, the reality is that even related subcomponents can differ widely from one another (Finkler et al., 2013). By examining components and subcomponents that are linked or reported together, it is possible to determine whether one part of the budget or related areas make up the largest variances. It may be the case that a large variance is being caused by faulty forecasting in only one part of the budget. By examining variances systematically and in parts, the P-12 budget manager can be assured that valuable time and resources are not being used inefficiently (Finkler et al., 2013).

Finally, because forecasting allows P-12 budget managers to make decisions about the future state of affairs, P-12 budget managers should strive to make variances between the forecasted and observed values as small as possible. Knowing where in the budget large variances occur is only the first step. The next step is to determine if these variances are a result of the cyclical nature of education finance or if structural elements have changed resulting in a need to rethink forecasting assumptions.

OVERSIGHT AND THE ROLE OF CYCLICAL AND STRUCTURAL VARIANCES

In the budget oversight process, an important distinction to make when examining the difference between observed and forecasted values is whether the resulting variance is due to cyclical forces or a structural change. When variances are due to a change in the budget environment that is either anticipated or that happens on a regular basis, P-12 budget managers should focus attention on how best to deal with the variance based on historical knowledge and local context.

Usually, a good course of action for cyclical budget variances is to reference policy for these anticipated fluctuations. In the event that a policy is not in place, the development of budget stabilization policies should look to smooth revenues or expenditures over this time so as to minimize differences between actual and anticipated values. Additionally, prudent use of cash reserves, when available, could help mitigate some of the difficulties that arise when cyclical variances occur.

If smoothing is not an option, then P-12 budget managers should try to anticipate which time periods will result in higher revenues or increased expenditures based on the business cycle. For example, while a P-12 budget manager may not be able to perfectly anticipate the number of sick days the teaching staff in a specific school will need in the month of October, having a plan for dealing with a significant difference between forecasted and actual funds for substitutes is wise and should be based on data regarding sick leave usage in the past. In other words, examining variances in revenues and expenditures from previous periods based on contextual knowledge of previous funding cycles and levels could provide a guide for dealing with budget fluctuations.

Once again, the use of cash reserves in an appropriate fashion could alleviate some of the pressures that build when variances occur. For example, it may be the case that reserves have been used in a similar manner in previous periods, and this can provide some guidance for the current period. In fact, the techniques presented in this chapter can be employed in the examination of the use and cyclicality of cash reserves as well.

Another good example of seasonal cyclicality comes from physical plant maintenance. Say, for example, that utility costs are estimated based on a 12-month figure, so that the value for each month is the same. However, it is more likely that utility costs will be higher during the time period that the physical plant is used most. In this instance, the P-12 budget manager might have negative variances for nine months and positive variances for three months. Locally, the reasons for this are clear; however, when a budget document is examined as a whole, these variances might raise questions. Since the P-12 budget managers know that the cyclical nature of the physical plant's use accounts for this variance, they are in a position to appropriately address concerns that the organization is running deficits some months and surpluses in others.

Now let's turn to structural variances. Structural variances arise when there is a change to the actual structure of the budget, its rules, or its policy. Structural variances differ from cyclical variances in that they are related to the structure of the budget process rather than to its fluctuations. A good example of this could be a state rescission, where the state alters the per pupil funding that school districts receive mid-school year due to a decrease in actual tax revenues.

The P-12 budget manager who faces this type of structural variance will need to alter the remaining periods of the school district budget despite all of the fixed costs. For example, school district officials are not going to dismiss a nontenured teacher if the rescission occurs in January. Instead, officials will make cuts in other areas of the budget and consider using cash reserve funds to make up any difference between the cuts and the fixed costs.

Variance analysis could indicate very different values based on the structural requirements and embedded assumptions of the budget process. Therefore, it is prudent for P-12 budget managers to understand clearly whether the variances they estimate are of a cyclical nature or a structural one. Speaking directly to the subject of cash reserves, in this case, these funds usually provide a buffer during the time period when policy, budgeting, or organizational changes must be made to deal with new structural constraints and opportunities. It is usually ill-advised to assume that cash reserves can shield the institution from structural changes over the long run.

VARIANCE ANALYSIS USING SUMMARY MEASURES

In this section, we outline the most common methods for examining variances among forecasted revenues and costs when compared to actual values using summary measures of the error. The exposition of these methods is guided by examples from Dunn (2012), Stevenson (2015), and Trochim and Donnelly (2007). By providing perspectives from three areas, policy analysis, operations management, and statistics, we are able to provide a step-by-step guide for carrying out typical variance analyses for P-12 budget managers needing summary measures of forecast accuracy.

It should be noted that because the measures employ error as a summary measure of forecasting accuracy, the goal is always to have smaller, rather than larger, variances. For the examples in this chapter, we will use the following dataset for per pupil expenditure over the last 20 time periods.[1]

Standard Error of Estimate

The standard error of estimate, or S_e, is a measure of the accuracy of prediction when using regression analysis for forecasting. It allows the budget manager to determine whether data points for both the actual and forecasted values are closely scattered near the line of best fit. The first step in this process is to plot the values and then impose a linear trend based on the forecasted results as shown in Figure 7.1.

This simple scatter plot shows that the forecasted and actual values move in a relatively similar fashion to one another and are rather closely grouped around the line of best fit. As noted in chapter 3, this should be done before

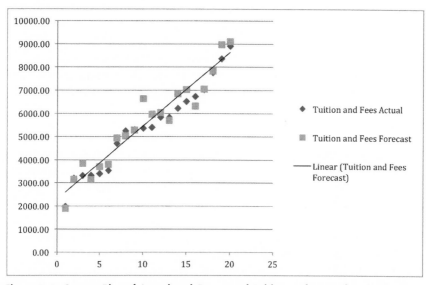

Figure 7.1   Scatter Plot of Actual and Forecasted Tuition and Fee Values with Linear Trend Superimposed. *Source*: Authors.

forecasting to determine if a linear forecasting trend makes sense. In this case it does. While this graphic shows us that the scatter appears close to the line, we may want to be able to quantify this in dollar terms to determine how far off the estimate is based on the distance between the actual and forecasted values. The standard error of estimate is calculated using the following equation (Stevenson, 2015, p. 103; Dunn, 2012, p. 103), where a sample of time periods has been taken:

$$S_e = \sqrt{\frac{\Sigma(y_a - y_f)^2}{n-2}}.$$

Here, the actual per pupil expenditure values (y_a) are subtracted from the forecasted ones (y_f), squared and then summed, in that order.[2] The numerator is then divided by the total number of observations (n) minus two. We then take the square root of this value for an estimate of the standard error. We should highlight that when calculating the S_e with an entire population of values (every period), it is not necessary to divide by $n - 2$ but rather only by n (Dunn, 2012).[3]

To make this discussion about standard error more concrete, we will take the equation and plug in values from Table 7.1, where we first subtract each actual value from the forecasted value and square the result. The equation is:

$$S_e = \sqrt{\frac{(3,859,429.54)}{20-2}} = 463.05.$$

To interpret this statistic, we need to construct a probability interpretation. So using a 95% confidence level, which is typical, the S_e indicates that 95% of the time the forecasted per pupil expenditure is within ±$926.10 tuition and fee dollars of the mean observed value.[4] Dunn (2012, p. 162) highlighted the power of this technique:

> The standard error of estimate allows us to make estimates that take error into account. Rather than make simple point estimates-that is, estimates that yield values of Y_c [Forecasted values of Y]- we can make interval estimates that yield values of Y_c expressed in terms of one or more standard units of error.

In other words, we can expect forecasts to be within this range or above or below the actual mean of tuition and fees a certain percentage of the time. Additionally, while the current example employs a revenue source for exposition, this applies equally well to expenditure forecasts, enrollments, and other components of a typical P-12 school district or school budget.

Table 7.1 Hypothetical Dataset with Actual, Forecasted, and Variance Values on Per Pupil Expenditure

School Year	Per Pupil Expenditure Actual (y_a)	Per Pupil Expenditure Forecast (y_f)	Variance (y_a-y_f)	Variance Squared $(y_a-y_f)^2$	Absolute Value of Variance $\lvert e \rvert$
1994–1995	1989.20	1904.89	84.31	7108.18	84.31
1995–1996	3198.75	3157.22	41.54	1725.57	41.54
1996–1997	3312.53	3841.08	−528.55	279365.10	528.55
1997–1998	3326.74	3131.44	195.30	38412.09	195.30
1998–1999	3399.78	3705.05	−305.26	93183.67	305.26
1999–1900	3533.82	3796.14	−262.32	68811.78	262.32
2000–2001	4706.70	4946.81	−240.11	57652.81	240.11
2001–2002	5248.03	5039.94	208.09	43301.45	208.09
2002–2003	5306.23	5288.59	17.64	311.17	17.64
2003–2004	5363.51	6640.95	−1277.44	1631852.95	1277.44
2004–2005	5403.13	5966.97	−563.84	317915.55	563.84
2005–2006	5833.94	6031.24	−197.30	38927.29	197.30
2006–2007	5833.94	5701.17	132.76	17625.22	132.76
2007–2008	6221.86	6850.37	−628.50	395012.25	628.50
2008–2009	6514.96	7040.69	−525.72	276381.52	525.72
2009–2010	6734.66	6318.84	415.82	172906.27	415.82
2010–2011	7029.66	7051.69	−22.02	484.88	22.02
2011–2012	7755.49	7835.65	−80.16	6425.63	80.16
2012–2013	8359.46	8969.99	−610.53	372746.88	610.53
2013–2014	8903.04	9101.90	−198.87	39549.28	198.87
Σ	**107975.45**	**112320.61**	**−4345.16**	**3859429.54**	**6536.08**

The first question that probably comes to mind is whether the ±$926.10 is acceptable, too large, or too small. The reality is that it depends. In this example, the S_e suggests that the deviation from the mean is not so large. Especially since the mean of the actual values is equal to 5398.77. This indicates that it is likely that the forecasting assumptions and model are working well. What is more, the S_e is directly related to the mean of observed values and thus, contextual knowledge about what may be too large, too small, or acceptable, is vital. This again underscores the important role of human judgment in tandem with sophisticated methods to obtain worthwhile forecasts (Finkler et al., 2013).

To be clear, the usefulness of the S_e lies in its ability to help the P-12 budget manager determine if forecasts and actual values are closely grouped because it depends on a more sophisticated forecasting approach (regression analysis) to determine the next forecasted value. It also expresses numerically the interval of error (at a 95% confidence level) that can be expected most of the time when predicting revenues and expenditures. Therefore, coupling local knowledge with appropriate forecasting approaches and assumptions can provide the P-12 budget manager essential information for decision-making and resource deployment.

Mean Absolute Deviation

The mean absolute deviation (MAD) is the average absolute forecast error (Stevenson, 2015, p. 81). It is the absolute value of the difference between each value and the mean of the dataset. So, in general, the equation for calculating the MAD is (Stevenson, 2015, p. 81):

$$\text{MAD} = \frac{\Sigma |e|}{n}.$$

Here, the *e* within the two brackets is the absolute value of the error (actual values minus forecasted values) divided by the total number of data points (*n*). To illustrate, let's use the data from Table 7.1 with the last six school years (school year 2008–2009 to school year 2013–2014). Based on the information from the table, it is observable that the difference between each forecast and the actual value has been calculated in column four, and the absolute values of these numbers are reported in column five, which must be calculated before proceeding. Because the bottom row of Table 7.1 includes these values for all 20 periods, we will have to calculate the MAD for the last six periods. To do so we set up the equation using data from the last column containing the absolute variance values:

$$\text{MAD} = \frac{525.72 + 415.82 + 22.02 + 80.16 + 610.53 + 198.87}{6} = 308.853.$$

This value, 308.853, provides a measure of average absolute distance between the data points and the mean of the sample. When the MAD is large it indicates that the data points are more scattered around the mean, and when small that they are more closely clustered around the mean. As underscored earlier, closer clustering around the mean suggests that forecasts are more accurate.

Given that this measure is a mean measure of the error, it is again necessary to determine what large and small mean in context. In this example, a MAD of 308.853 for the actual value of tuition and fees could suggest that observable variances are relatively small given that the actual values range from a high of 8,903.04 to a low of 6,514.96. Hence, this may indicate that forecasting assumptions are acceptable. However, if we compared the value 308.853 to a high of 890.30 and a low of 651.49, then this MAD would be rather large and could indicate that a revisiting of forecasting assumptions is required. Finally, it is important to note that this approach is relatively simple to employ; however, it also makes assumptions about the error; namely, it weights the error linearly, which imposes a strict assumption about forecasted values (Stevenson, 2015).

Mean Squared Error

In terms of summarizing the accuracy of a forecast, the mean squared error (MSE) is often considered to be one of the most powerful tools at an analyst's disposal. MSE is a good measure of the precision and accuracy of a forecast based on historical data (SAS/STAT (R), 2009). In mathematical terms, MSE is denoted by the following equation (Stevenson, 2015, p. 81):

$$MSE = \frac{\Sigma e^2}{n-1}.$$

In this equation, the MSE is equal to the sum of the squared errors[5] divided the number of observations minus one. For example, if we use per pupil expenditure data as in the previous example with the six most recent school years, the equation would take the following form again using the absolute values of the forecast error:

$$MSE = \frac{525.72^2 + 415.82^2 + 22.02^2 + 80.16^2 + 610.53^2 + 198.87^2}{5} = 173,698.89.$$

Now this number may seem enormous and, in fact, it is. Therefore, a good approach is simply to take the square root of the MSE to obtain the root mean squared error (RMSE). By doing so we can interpret the MSE in the original units. So in this example, that would mean taking the square root (173,698.89) for a value of 416.77. This is interpreted in the original units (per pupil expenditure) and used in much the same way as the MAD when comparing the RMSE to the actual values to determine if it is too large or too small (Vernier, 2011), with larger numbers implying greater forecasting inaccuracy. It should be highlighted that the RMSE is also used in control charts, which are explained in this chapter, to provide both tracking information and visual information related to forecast accuracy.

This method is very useful and can provide a sophisticated summary measure of the forecast variance. However, like other methods, it also suffers from a rather important limitation. Primarily, that the use of squared errors results in larger weights for larger errors so that when the difference between the actual and forecasted values are large, these values are given heavier weighting. This can lead to problems with both precision and bias in forecast estimates and hence should be considered carefully when in use (SAS/STAT(R), 2009; Stevenson, 2015).

Mean Absolute Percentage Error

The mean absolute percentage error (MAPE) is the value of the average absolute percent error. Essentially, this measures forecasting accuracy in percentage terms as opposed to original units. The equation for calculating the MAPE is as follows (Stevenson, 2015, p. 81):

$$\text{MAPE} = \frac{\Sigma\left[\frac{|e|}{y_a} \times 100\right]}{n}.$$

Here, the numerator is equal to the sum of the absolute values of the error terms (e) divided by the actual forecast for each included period multiplied by 100. Let's assume that we will again do this analysis for the most recent six school years from the dataset reported in Table 7.1. The calculations and values are reported in Table 7.2.

The values in the last column of Table 7.2 are calculated by taking the absolute variance value ($|e|$) from each time period and dividing it by its corresponding actual values (y_a). Therefore, to obtain the value 8.07% for school year 2008–2009, we simply calculate (525.72/6,514.96) × 100. The same is done for each time period. So for school year 2009–2010, the equation to be calculated would be (415.82/6,734.66) × 100 = 6.17%. Once again, we have calculated all of these values for each time period they are summed, and we have the value 25.13%. In order to obtain the MAPE, we simply plug in these values as such:

$$\text{MAPE} = \frac{25.13\%}{6} = 4.19\%.$$

The resulting value of 4.19% suggests that the forecast is off by a little more than 4% for the periods included in the calculation. This does not appear to be a very large amount, and based on previous calculations of the MSE and MAD, it would seem that the P-12 budget manager is doing a rather good job at forecasting future per pupil expenditure revenues.[6]

As has been highlighted in previous sections, summary measures of forecast accuracy provide a great deal of useful information, and the MAPE is

Table 7.2   Hypothetical Dataset with Actual, Forecasted, Variance, and Percentages*

School Year	Per Pupil Expenditure Actual (y_a)	Per Pupil Expenditure Forecast (y_f)	Variance ($y_a - y_f$)	Absolute Value of Variance $|e|$	$(|e| \div y_a)$* 100 (%)
2008–2009	6514.96	7040.69	−525.72	525.72	8.07
2009–2010	6734.66	6318.84	415.82	415.82	6.17
2010–2011	7029.66	7051.69	−22.02	22.02	0.31
2011–2012	7755.49	7835.65	−80.16	80.16	1.03
2012–2013	8359.46	8969.99	−610.53	610.53	7.30
2013–2014	8903.04	9101.9	−198.87	198.87	2.23
				$\Sigma =$	25.13

*Note: That in the case of the default credit rating S&P maintains one rating more than does Moody's.

not different in this sense. It provides information that can put the error in perspective (Stevenson, 2015) so that errors are understood in percentage terms rather than simply as units. It does, however, suffer from a rather important limitation, chiefly that it does not deal well with near-zero or actual zero values. This is a result of its mechanics, which render the value of the MAPE undefined.

APPROACH FOR OVERSIGHT AND MONITORING OF FORECAST VARIANCE

In the previous section, the goal was to outline the most common methods of examining forecast variance using summary measures of the error. In this section, we outline the most common method of tracking forecast variance rather than simply measuring it. Following Stevenson (2015), we provide detailed examples and step-by-step instructions for using a control chart approach. As in the previous section, the examples used here employ the dataset for per pupil expenditure over the last 20 school years presented in Table 7.1 with a few changes based on what is needed for each approach.

We should also underscore that we have chosen not to provide a detailed exposition of another method of monitoring forecast accuracy, tracking signal, because recent advances in computing power have resulted in the use of the more sophisticated approach presented in this section. Moreover, using a tracking signal to examine forecast accuracy is severely limited by its focus upon cumulative rather than individual errors. The approach does not consider each error individually but rather relies on cumulative values that can obscure individual outliers important to the analysis (Stevenson, 2015).

Control Chart

This method is used for tacking forecast accuracy by identifying possible nonrandomness in forecasting errors (Stevenson, 2015). By using the equivalent of what would be the mean for an error (0) and standard deviation-MSE, the control chart provides a visual and sophisticated means of tracking errors using the basic probabilities outlined in the section titled "Standard Error of Estimate" (see footnote 3). Because we assume that this is a sample of possible periods, when calculating the MSE we should use the $n - 1$ convention to help reduce bias in our estimates (see Table 7.3).

The computation and creation of a control chart requires a great deal of data and computing assistance. Using Excel, this task, however, becomes much easier.[7] For example, in Figure 7.2 a control chart example is provided in an Excel screenshot.

Table 7.3   Control Chart Data

School Year	Variance (Error)	Error Squared
1994–1995	84.31	7108.82
1995–1996	41.54	1725.22
1996–1997	−528.55	279365.25
1997–1998	195.30	38142.93
1998–1999	−305.26	93184.73
1999–2000	−262.32	68812.83
2000–2001	−240.11	57652.91
2001–2002	208.09	43302.73
2002–2003	17.64	311.23
2003–2004	−1277.44	1631843.21
2004–2005	−563.84	317912.89
2005–2006	−197.30	38927.99
2006–2007	132.76	17626.02
2007–2008	−628.50	395016.38
2008–2009	−525.72	276385.99
2009–2010	415.82	172905.37
2010–2011	−22.02	485.08
2011–2012	−80.16	6425.20
2012–2013	−610.53	372752.06
2013–2014	−198.87	39547.50
Σ		3859434.35
MSE		203128.12
RMSE		450.70

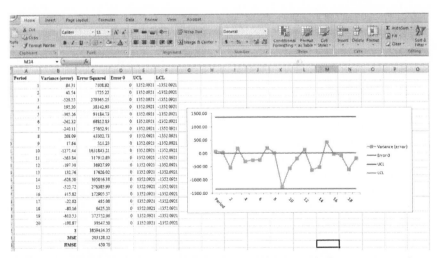

Figure 7.2   Excel Screen Shot of Data Requirements for Control Chart. *Source*: Authors.

To start with, the P-12 budget manager will need to calculate the MSE using the technique presented earlier in this chapter and find its square root (s). This measure works similar to the computation of a standard deviation but is specifically for measuring the distribution of error terms. Following Stevenson's (2015, p. 107) approach we need to compute the following values:

$$s = \sqrt{\text{MSE}}.$$

$$\text{Upper Control Limit}\left(\text{UCL}\right) = 0 + z * s.$$

$$\text{Lower Control Limit}\left(\text{LCL}\right) = 0 - z * s.$$

Here, s is equal to the square root of the MSE, and z is equal to the number of standard deviations away from the mean (of the error values) that are statistically acceptable assuming normality of the distribution. So, in this case, 68% of errors are expected to fall within one standard deviation, 95% within two standard deviations, and 99% within three. In other words, the budget manager must set the "limit" on what is acceptably within the upper and lower limits. So, in the example provided in Figure 7.2, first we calculate the square root of the MSE, which results in:

$$s = \sqrt{203,128.12} = 450.70.$$

The UCL limit is calculated with three standard deviations as:

$$\text{UCL} = 0 + 3\left(450.70\right) = 1,352.0921 \ or \ 1,352.1,$$

and the LCL as:

$$\text{LCL} = 0 - 3\left(450.70\right) = -1,352.0921 \ or \ -1,352.1.$$

This information is plotted in Figure 7.3. The reason for plotting these values is that it quickly shows that per pupil expenditure, from a statistically significant perspective, is within acceptable limits if three standard deviations are used. Instead, if two standard deviations were considered to be the limit, then we would use the same equations and come up with ± 901.40. To help make this clearer, let's turn to deciphering Figure 7.3.

In Figure 7.3, we see four lines on the graph. The darkest line at the top near 1,500 is the UCL, the lighter line near the bottom (−1,500) is the LCL, and the line in the straight line in the middle is the center of the range of random variability based on a normal distribution. The jagged line with the squares is the one connecting each of the variance or error values. It is

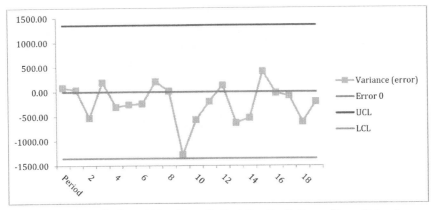

Figure 7.3 Control Chart Using Hypothetical Per Pupil Expenditure Data. *Source:* Example adapted from Stevenson, 2015.

important to emphasize what the control chart shows; namely, it provides visual information about the spread of forecasting errors.

Based on the control chart presented in Figure 7.3, it is clear that all values fall within the UCL and LCL; though one comes pretty close to being beyond the lower limit. While this is good news, the reality is that we must consider not only the limits, but the shape of the line as well. The UCL and LCL are only one measure of the spread of forecasting error. Other things to look for include trends in the variance line, cycling, and bias (Stevenson, 2015).

For example, there does not appear to be any discernible trend either upward or downward, but cycles do seem to be at play here. This could indicate that during certain times, the forecasts are off in a cyclical pattern suggesting that we may not be considering important external factors such as changes in political dynamics around education finance, or increased competition from other institutions.

Additionally, the control chart shows that many of the forecasting errors fall below the centerline. This suggests that the forecasting estimates are biased upward (e.g., actual per pupil expenditure = 10,500, forecasted per pupil expenditure = 11,600, variance is −1,100) and that the budget manager may need to reexamine the internal and external environments as well as the assumptions going into each forecast for changes impacting actual versus forecasted values.

AUDIT, ACCOUNTABILITY, AND TRANSPARENCY

Another important function of budget oversight and variance analysis is related to accountability and transparency. Finkler et al. (2013) noted that safeguarding resources is an important function of the oversight process and provide four items that should be considered as part of both the oversight and the audit process. These are summarized here:

1. A management authorization system should be in place so that key activities are carried out only with proper management approval
2. After authorization is secured, all budgetary and financial transactions should be carefully recorded in preparation for financial statements and to ensure accountability for all resources and assets
3. Only those with proper management authority should have access to assets and resources
4. Reconciliation of current assets and resources, and those recorded previously, should occur on a regular basis and differences should be reconciled. (p. 287)

These are clearly only the most basic components of an audit system[8] and set the foundation for a comprehensive audit trail; however, they are extremely important. Moreover, the public nature of P-12 education means that transparency around financial and budget administration is essential.

As noted by Barr and McClellan (2011a, b), oversight of budgets and audits can come from both internal and external sources. For example, most school districts are required, as per state law, to conduct internal audits to maintain proper oversight and adherence to the audit and control system in place. Additionally, school districts, as part of their mission to be accountable to tax payers, are audited by the state. Moreover, school districts that take part in federal grant are required to undergo an audit by the federal government (Goldstein, 2012).[9] Similarly, all school districts are required to undergo an audit conducted by an external agency. This helps to ensure that a review of institutional fiscal operations and administration is carried out independently.

Finally, while the audit process is typically intended to provide information about appropriate resources management, highlight weaknesses in the process, and strengthen budget procedures, the results of an audit are not necessarily confined to internal uses (Barr & McClellan, 2011a, b). In fact, for school districts, state-level audits are often made public for the sake of transparency and accountability. Hence, the publicness of audits means that the school district officials should take special care to steer clear of preventable inaccuracies that result from poor oversight or careless budgetary procedures (Barr & McClellan, 2011a, b). While we have underscored the extra scrutiny faced by public institutions, in reality, all institutions should heed the advice provided here.

CONCLUSION

Analysis of budget variances and appropriate oversight are central components of strong fiscal administration. This chapter has provided myriad examples and methods for examining budget variances. It has also highlighted the important role of oversight and its relationship to accountability and transparency. As higher education serves a public function, scrutiny of fiscal operations should not be avoided. Indeed, special care must be taken to guarantee that resources and assets are safeguarded and that they are being used appropriately. In this chapter, we have provided the budget manager the tools to do so.

GUIDING QUESTIONS

The following questions address many of the key concepts covered in chapter 7. Readers should be able to answer these questions upon completing the chapter:

1. What general purpose does variance analysis serve for the P-12 budget manager?
2. Briefly describe how structural variances and cyclical variances differ from one another.
3. How do forecast variances aid P-12 budget managers with oversight and monitoring?

ADDITIONAL READING

Those readers desiring additional information on the concepts addressed in chapter 7 should consult the following:

Finkler, S., R. Purtell, T. Calabrese, & D. Smith. 2013. *Financial management for public, health, and not-for-profit organizations* (4th ed.). Upper Saddle River, NJ: Pearson.

EXERCISES

The following exercises are designed to provide readers opportunities to take the concepts addressed in chapter 7 and apply them using actual data.

Table 7.4   Fictional Dataset for Variance Analysis

School Year	Per Pupil Expenditure Actual (y_a)	Per Pupil Expenditure Forecasted (y_f)
1994–1995	2557.46	2172.85
1995–1996	2688.30	2207.55
1996–1997	3245.73	2678.30
1997–1998	3921.61	3040.08
1998–1999	3931.01	3378.16
1999–2000	4281.08	3412.76
2000–2001	4560.28	3433.83
2001–2002	5064.07	3920.62
2002–2-03	5637.17	5133.58
2003–2004	5745.11	5430.68
2004–2005	6024.17	5890.37
2005–2006	6494.71	6381.77
2006–2007	6495.92	6441.94
2007–2008	7227.13	6644.68
2008–2009	7806.97	7155.74
2009–2010	7981.96	7163.57
2010–2011	8167.25	8470.78
2011–2012	8348.33	8775.48
2012–2013	8453.10	8817.68
2013–2014	8684.09	9082.85

1. Using the dataset in Table 7.4, and Microsoft Excel if available, calculate each of the following summary measures for all 20 periods:
   a. Standard error of estimate
   b. Mean average deviation
   c. Mean square error
   d. Root mean square error
   e. Mean absolute percentage error
   Briefly describe how each measure should be understood.
2. Using Microsoft Excel and the dataset provided, create a control chart. Then answer the following questions:
   a. What does the visualization of data in the control charts represent?
   b. How does one go about interpreting the information?
   c. When should a budget manager become concerned by the data presented in a control chart?
   d. What if the control chart shows that values are close to but not outside the threshold limits? How might a new budget manager approach this?
   e. What if limits are only reached, or closely reached, for one time period? Should a full reexamination take place? What if this instead is happening consistently?

3. Briefly describe the fundamental components of an appropriate audit process

4. Describe how human judgment plays a role in forecasting for institutions of higher education.

NOTES

1. Periods can be any length of time, including day, week, month, semester, trimester, or year.

2. Readers should note that not following the proper order of operations will result in a very different and incorrect value for the numerator of the S_e.

3. Trochim and Donnelly (2007) suggested dividing by $n - 1$ instead of $n - 2$. However, the goal of both of these corrections is to estimate unbiased standard errors.

4. This value is calculated by multiplying the S_e by the number of standard deviations related to the confidence interval where the forecast will be within one standard deviation of the actual mean 68% of the time, within two standard deviations 95% of the time, and within three standard deviations 99% of the time. So we simply multiply 463.05×2 to construct the probability interpretation.

5. Readers may be confused by the fact that we do not employ the absolute value in this equation. The reason for doing so is that squaring the value of e results in positive numbers, which is the same logic behind using absolute values.

6. The appropriate measure of MAPE values is based upon local context and depends greatly upon the requirements of the organization. In some instances, a MAPE of less than 5% is acceptable whereas in others, a MAPE of less than 20% is acceptable.

7. For those unfamiliar with Excel for control charts, a great video tutorial exists from Eugene O'Loughlin (2012) at the National College of Ireland at https://www.youtube.com/watch?v=zvp8qmEos. This uses examples that are readily adaptable to the exercises presented here.

8. For a detailed description of the element of a control system, see Finkler et al. (2013, pp. 287–93).

9. Goldstein (2012, p. 18) highlights that fact that Office of Management and Budget Circulars A-110 and A-133 govern the audit process for the audit of federally funded programs.

Phase III

CAPITAL PROJECTS WITH AND WITHOUT DEBT

In this phase of the book, we present some important budget components and considerations beyond those that have already been discussed. Specifically, we are interested in providing readers with an overview of the capital budgeting process (both with and without debt), the basics of time value of money, and cost–benefit analysis tools. We then move on to the role of the strategic plan in budgeting, and how the aggregation of both the operating and capital budgets constitutes the "master budget." This master budget is highly influential in the planning process because it outlines the overall goals and objectives of the institution in financial terms. What is more, the master budget is a manifestation of the previous planning processes, and a starting point for future plans. It is the relationship between budgets and planning that is the focus of chapter 10. The final chapter of this phase offers some concluding remarks and perspectives on major trends in the field.

Chapter 8

Capital Budgets without Debt

The capital budget serves to facilitate the acquisition and financial management of long-term physical assets and other assets that last for more than one operating year (Finkler et al., 2013; Lee, Johnson, & Joyce, 2013). In P-12 public education, the majority of capital budgets deal with the maintenance, renovation, repair, replacement, or new construction of physical plant (buildings, classrooms, lab space, student centers, etc.), large transportation expenditures, or technology system upgrades (Barr & McClellan, 2011b). In order to pay for these amenities and other large capital acquisitions, P-12 administrators must use capital budgets to plan how funds will be allocated across these activities over many years.

Why is a separate budget needed to deal with these types of expenditures? The capital budget allows for institutions to repay the cost of these asset types over the useful life of the asset through a process called amortization (Finkler et al., 2013). The amortization principle allows for fiscal managers to budget the day-to-day operation of the asset over a longer period of time and account only for related costs to be included in the operating budget under "depreciation" in the financial statements (Finkler et al., 2013). This is done so long as the asset remains useful, or in operation.

In addition, this process means that multiple future school years are part of the budgeting process when dealing with capital assets. Finally, the state policymaker or the school district official must establish guidelines regarding dollar limits for those items to be included in the capital budget. For example, Finkler et al. (2013, p. 165) suggested that capital expenditures should typically require a significant outlay of resources and be useful and owned for a long period of time.

Generally speaking, the capital budgeting process includes only six steps as outlined by Goldstein (2012, pp. 129–31), which are presented in Table 8.1

in three stages. We should note that while the focus of this chapter is on capital budgeting without debt, the same process holds for capital budgeting with debt. Additionally, the same notions around the useful life and policies for determining what should be considered a capital asset apply.

As can be seen in Table 8.1, when compared with the operating budget the capital budget cycle has fewer stages and steps; however, one should not take this to indicate that the budget cycle is less complicated or shorter. In fact, as compared with the operating budget, the capital budget deals with fiscal administration and budgeting over a much longer period of years (Goldstein, 2012).

While the data in Table 8.1 provide a broad overview of the process, as with other budgeting and financial decisions, the local context should always be considered. That is to say, as with the ebbs and flows related to the operating budget, both internal and external factors impacting the process should be considered when undertaking capital budgeting. In addition, the process outlined earlier points to an important part of the capital budget process— that the financial impact of large acquisitions is only truly understood over the useful life of the asset. Because this is the case, the time value of money (TVM) plays an important role in determining the best use of capital funds (Finkler et al., 2013; Lee et al., 2013).

Another important part of the capital budgeting process that is not included in Table 8.1 is the relationship of the capital budget to the total program of the school district. While the process outlined earlier explains how the acquisition of big-ticket items proceeds, it does little to tell us about the impact of capital investments and acquisitions on the other part of the "master budget," the operating side. For the most part, capital budgets impact total program budgets in at least four ways.

First, there are often operating costs associated with increased faculty or staff when a project is completed. This directly impacts the operating budget by increasing the day-to-day costs of running a school. Second, once the project is brought online, it will require maintenance funding. While many capital projects require some reserve to deal with this part of the process, it is not always the case that these will cover the full costs of operation especially as external variables fluctuate. In a related vein, the costs of depreciation are dealt with on the operating side.

The third way capital projects impact a school district's total program is if the institution chooses to employ debt, there is the matter of debt service. The costs of paying back the debt plus interest are decidedly part of the operating budget. Finally, when new space is added to a school, then there is a cost associated with furnishing it with all of the necessary materials like desks, computers, and textbooks. All of these considerations are part of prudent fiscal administration and should be part of capital budgeting decisions.

Table 8.1 Example Operating Budget Cycle for a School District over Four Fiscal Years

Stage in Cycle	Task	Timeline (Fiscal Year July 1–June 30)	Description
Classroom space needs and campus plans	Determine classroom space requirements	School Year/Fiscal Year 1	This part of the process will include building and central office administration and maintenance personnel and should include a rationale for space needs.
	Determine if space is already available on campus	School Year/Fiscal Year 1	This includes looking for possible reassignment of space but should be done with the least disruption possible.
	Review the school district's strategic and master building plans	School Year/Fiscal Years 1–2	In this step, the goal is to assess the appropriateness of the new or renovated spaces goals and objectives with those of the strategic and master building plans.
Feasibility and approval	Determine if the proposed projects are feasible	School Year/Fiscal Years 2–3	This component should examine the need for space as related to other requests and rationales for additional or new space as well as necessary time commitments if the project is undertaken.
	Get the right approvals and secure the financial plan to pay for the project	School Year/Fiscal Year 2	For school districts, it is likely that more than the school board will have input into the process and final approval.
Build or acquire	Make the purchase or build the space	School Year/Fiscal Years 3–4	Once the preceding steps have been taken, it is then time to either build the space or purchase the item. Although this seems relatively straightforward, this may take many years and involve budget complications.

Now that we are a bit more familiar with the process of capital budgeting, the next step is to understand how school district officials can go about financing large projects or acquisitions. As there are a number of possible alternatives for acquiring capital assets, we will focus on those not needing debt in this chapter. Again, this does not necessarily change the decision-making process in terms of the final choice of acquisition, but it can certainly impact the fiscal sustainability and positioning of the institution.

FUNDING NEW PROJECTS WITHOUT DEBT

In P-12 public education, there are a number of ways to pay for capital investments that do not require the issuance of debt, although in recent years the tendency of school districts to employ debt for capital projects has been on the rise (Jacob, Stange, & McCall, 2013; Serna, 2013). We, nonetheless, wish to highlight the funding mechanisms available to P-12 school districts seeking to fund capital projects without issuing a bond. We wish to focus on the alternatives available to school districts and to illustrate some of their limitations.

Capital Fund-Raising and Campaigns

Capital fund-raising and campaigns are examples of what Barr and McClellan (2011a, b) call "focused giving." This type of fund-raising is directed at a specific project deemed of importance either in the school district's master building plan or strategic plan. Fund-raising has been part of P-12 public education, primarily in the area of athletics. However, capital campaigns could focus on raising funds for buildings or renovations. The reason a capital campaign is so attractive is that it has the added advantage of providing a large amount of funding for a project without requiring repayment or incurring debt costs.

While capital campaigns have some very attractive attributes, they also come with some significant limitations. First, this type of fund-raising is restricted only to the project for which it is raised. In other words, if the project is not undertaken or ends with a surplus of funds, these monies cannot be shifted to another budgeting category or priority (Finkler et al., 2013).

Second, development offices might find that donors are less willing or able to donate to other important areas. Third, raising money for a capital acquisition that is a school district or school priority can take a great deal of time and energy. It is not unusual for capital campaigns to last many years before raising the needed funds. As school district officials determine the capital needs, this should be part of the deliberation process. That is to say, if the capital needs of the school district are urgent, a capital campaign may not be the most expeditious way to raise funds.

Paygo and Usage of Fund Balances

Pay-as-you-go (Paygo) is a system of capital budgeting that pays for a capital projects out of currently available funds rather than issuing long-term debt. As with other approaches that do not employ debt, it is attractive because the school district does not have to pay interest costs. However, the Paygo approach does suffer from some rather important limitations.

The primary limitation of this approach is that it requires significant fore-thought around capital acquisitions and future needs. This approach requires that yearly capital expenditures remain fairly even from year to year (Lee, Johnson, & Joyce, 2013). If a school district can sufficiently forecast needed capital acquisitions and set aside monies from current funds to cover these expenditures, then Paygo is a viable approach.

However, most school districts require large, variable, and less predictable amounts of capital financing. Another significant limitation of this approach is that it requires that monies from current funding sources are used to finance capital projects. This means that school districts are required to make a trade-off regarding current spending and long-term benefits. In other words, school districts may have to spend less on other important operating functions in order to maintain a capital budget in this manner.

Moreover, Paygo is particularly difficult to maintain if economic condi-tions worsen or unexpected fluctuations in anticipated revenues or expen-ditures are seen. When fiscal conditions are volatile, capital budgets using Paygo may simply be sacrificed to make up for shortfalls occurring in other parts of the budget (Lee, Johnson, & Joyce, 2013).

Similar to Paygo, the usage of fund balances relies upon current funds. The difference, however, is that it relies upon excess funds from the operating budget after accounting for all liabilities and assets (Governmental Account-ing Standards Board, 2006). Assuming that these funds are not restricted, they can be employed to fund capital projects or acquisitions. However, the use of this funding source suffers from the same limitations outlined for Paygo approaches. Finally, and distinct from the Paygo approach, is that while Paygo deliberately sets aside funds for capital projects, the use of fund balances relies on monies that are left over from operating expenses and rev-enues, hence, making them less stable from year to year.

School district officials may also opt to annually set aside a portion of the funds for a capital project for a fixed number of years to ensure that in the desired time frame the funds are available for the building need. An example of this approach could include school district officials putting $15,000 into a cash reserve account annually and then buying a new school bus, which may cost between $52,000 and $60,000, every five years.

Another slight variation of this approach to Paygo is exemplified by a school district that was guaranteed to save over $100,000 annually after an extensive overhaul to its heating and cooling system in all of its buildings. The guaranteed savings were applied to a 10-year loan to cover the cost of the capital project, resulting in a net effect of zero on the total program since the savings covered the interest and principal loan payments.

There is a bit of an alarming trend in P-12 public education that merits reference in this section. Many of the Paygo capital projects are smaller in scale, as opposed to the building of a brand new school, for example, and have, historically, been covered financially as P-12 school district officials have set aside a small portion of the total program (typically a set amount of money for each student enrolled in the school district) for building upkeep and basic renovation. However, these basic capital projects are beginning to show up in multimillion-dollar bond proposals that must be approved by voters.

Once bonds with capital projects that could be covered by a Paygo approach are approved by voters, then all property owners within the boundaries of the school district are agreeing to not only pay for the capital project, but also pay interest on that capital project. In other words, a smaller capital project, like reroofing a high school that could cost roughly $600,000, funded through a voter-approved bond, could see the total cost, principal plus interest, nearly double to over $1,000,000.

TIME VALUE OF MONEY

In the process of capital budgeting, time plays an important role for decision-makers. This is because the value of money in the future is not the same as the value of money in the present and vice versa. To put it differently, just like $100 today is not the same as $100 about 50 years ago, $100 today is not worth the same amount as $100 about 50 years from today. The reason for this is that the further away the acquisition of a dollar amount is from the present the less it is worth in the present, and the longer an investment sits accruing interest the larger the amount will be.

As noted before, the true fiscal impact of a capital project or acquisition can only be understood in terms of its useful life. Because this is the case, the TVM plays an important role in determining how capital funds will be allocated, and also which projects provide the most benefits for the costs. In this section, we summarize some basic concepts related to the TVM and provide some examples of how it is used in practice.

Discounting and Compounding Basics

To start, let us examine how discounting works to provide us a proper valuation technique for making decisions about the present dollar value of some amount in the future. Following Dunn (2012, pp. 229–33) and Finkler et al. (2013, pp. 167–71), we would employ the following equation to determine the present discounted value (*PV*) of monies stated in future terms:

$$PV = \frac{FV}{(1+i)^N}.$$

In order to employ this equation correctly, we will require a few pieces of information. First, let us assume that school district officials have decided that it will enhance student learning by providing extra tutoring space on campus. School district officials are able to spend $25,000 on the space today (an outlay) and will receive this money back in three years from a voter-approved mill levy override. However, this budgeting decision does not account for the difference in time between the outlay and the recouping of costs. In order for the transaction to make sense, the P-12 budget manager must account for time in the decision-making process. To do so requires the use of the equation presented earlier.

To make this more concrete, assume that the total number of discount periods[1] away from the present is equal to three. Also, assume that the going market rate for borrowing is 5%. With this information we have enough data to determine how much $25,000 three years from now would be worth in today's dollars. If we insert these values into the *PV* equation, we get:

$$PV = \frac{\$25,000}{(1+0.05)^3} \ or \approx \$21,596.$$

Hence, this equation indicates that the present discounted value of $25,000 received three years from now would actually only cover $21,596 of the project. Another way to approach this is by calculating the discount factor (*DF*) using the approach laid out by Dunn (2012, p. 231):

$$DF = \frac{1}{(1+r)^n}.$$

This is done with an equation that provides u It is also very close to the value s with a factor for discounting any amount using information about the market interest rate (*r*) and number of periods (*n*) for which the values must be discounted or compounded. For this example, it would look like:

$$DF = \frac{1}{(1+.05)^3} \ or \approx 0.8638.$$

Doing so would allow the budget manager to use this discount rate for any value, not just the $25,000 in our example with close approximation. Say, for example, that a capital project requires an outlay of $150,000, and the market rate, as well as the number of periods, remains the same. Using the *DF*, this calculation is simple:

$$\$150,000 \times .8638 = \$129,570.$$

It is also very close to the value obtained from the *PV* equation earlier ($129,575.64).

If the fiscal manager had some leeway to negotiate for the full amount required to cover the total cost of the tutoring services, then this requires the use of the following equation for the calculation of future compounded value (*FV*).

$$FV = PV(1+i)^N.$$

So in a similar fashion, this requires the same information as the *PV* equation. To do so, insert the needed values into the equation to come up with:

$$FV = 25,000(1+.05)^3 \ or \approx \$28,941.$$

This indicates that in order to fully cover the costs of this capital outlay would require $28,941 in three years as opposed to $25,000.

The reason for this larger value is that it is assumed that money today could be invested at the market rate and because of compounding, or the process of earning interest on interest earned, can grow more quickly. This basic assumption is what accounts for the difference in the terms of *PV* as compared with *FV*. Another important consideration for *FV*, or compounding, is that interest may not be paid on a yearly basis. In fact, many investments pay biannually or quarterly.

To illustrate, suppose that the school district has decided that it will undertake the tutoring services project on in three years and has $25,000 today that it can invest today to pay for the project.[2] Based on the earlier example it is clear that with interest and compounding paid yearly this would result in a return of $28,941. But what happens if interest is not compounded annually but instead is compounded twice a year? This requires a reworking of the *FV* equation to reflect this fact.

The *FV* equation's interest rate has to be divided by the number of compound periods in a year and the number of periods increased. In this case, the total number of periods would rise from three to six and the interest rate would go from 5% to 2.5%. This is necessary because of the way in which compounding works, namely, that the investment earns interest upon interest earned in previous periods.[3] Since the needed information is available, the next step is simply to plug in the new values into the *FV* equation:

$$FV = 25,000(1+.025)^6 \ or \approx \$28,992.$$

This example shows the power of compounding, in that the value over the same three-year period is increased slightly thanks to interest payments happening twice a year. If the same example were used with quarterly payments, the total amount in three years would total approximately $29,019. While these values may not seem very different, as both the number of interest payments per year and the number of years increase, this can have a very large impact on the *FV* of an amount invested today, especially when working with larger amounts of money.

Outlined in this section are the basic mechanics of the discounting and compounding. However, in day-to-day fiscal administration, it is not often the case that outlays and investments work out so smoothly. In the next section, we present the foundations of cost–benefit analysis as related to the TVM. We introduce the concept of net present value (NPV) and benefit/revenue streams and their relationship to decision-making as well as the compounding and discounting.

Annual Cash Flows and Choosing Projects

The previously outlined models used in the TVM calculations provide a fundamental process for making correct comparisons when outlays are required and/or investments are paid back at some single point in time. The limitation with these techniques, however, is that they do not allow for the inclusion of either annual payments or costs associated with a project.

A way to get around this limitation is to include these cash flows as part of the analysis. As a departure from previous chapters and sections, we employ a number of Excel screenshots given that the process for calculating many of the values in the next few sections are quite cumbersome when done using mathematical approaches that use formulas requiring yearly calculations. The formulas employed in this section are applicable to the *FV* and *PV* examples provided earlier, with the simple exclusion of the [pmt] portion of the Excel formula function.

Future Value with Annuities

Sometimes school district officials are able to set aside funds for some future project and may also find themselves in a position where it is possible to add to the initial investment. To illustrate, suppose that a school district wishes to replace computers in an elementary school in the near future. The antici-pated expenditure is expected to be just over $30,000. School district officials know that the elementary school does not have sufficient funds to pay for the technical upgrades, and the officials also know that the current systems will remain adequate for the next three years. In this case, assume that the school district officials wish to know how much $25,000 will be worth in three years if invested at 5%.

The school district officials also know that elementary school budget can add an additional $1,000 per year to the initial investment. Essentially, the school district is able to invest the principal but is also able to add to the principal amount during the investment period. Hence, if the principal is only invested, then the *FV* of the $25,000 would simply take on the values calculated previously in this chapter and would total approximately $28,941 if interest was compounded once a year.

With this in mind, however, we can now calculate what the *FV* of the prin-cipal plus additional monies would equal at the end of three years by using a modified *FV* equation. Because this formula becomes very cumbersome quickly, it is best presented as an Excel spreadsheet equation as in the screen-shots in Figures 8.1, 8.2, 8.3, and 8.4. The Excel formula for *FV* provides a space for all of the required information necessary for this calculation.

In Figure 8.2, we have plugged in the values for each required variable except [type]. A few notes about employing this formula in Excel are required before proceeding. First, when using the *FV* functionality in Excel, it is pos-sible to simply click on the cell (use cell references) to fill in the formula. This would result in Figure 8.3.

Regardless of how one chooses to input the information, the final calcula-tion should equal $32,093.13, as in Figure 8.4.

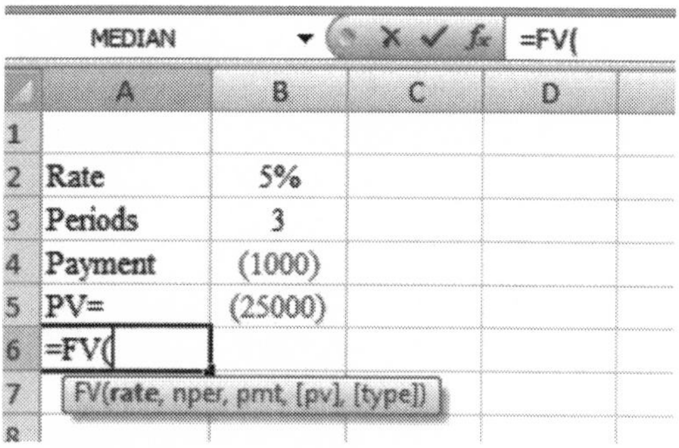

Figure 8.1   Excel Example 1. *Source:* Example adapted and expanded from Finkler et al., 2013.

MEDIAN		▼	× ✓ *fx*	=FV(.05, 3, -1000, -25000)	
	A	B	C	D	E	F
1						
2	Rate	5%				
3	Periods	3				
4	Payment	(1000)				
5	PV=	(25000)				
6	=FV(.05, 3, -1000, -25000)					

Figure 8.2 Excel Example 2. *Source*: Examples adapted and expanded from Finkler et al., 2013.

MEDIAN		▼	× ✓ *fx*	=FV(B2,B3,B4,B5)
	A	B	C	D	E
1					
2	Rate	5%			
3	Periods	3			
4	Payment	(1000)			
5	PV=	(25000)			
6	=FV(B2,B3,B4,B5)				
7	FV(rate, nper, pmt, **[pv]**, [type])				

Figure 8.3 Excel Example 3. *Source*: Example adapted and expanded from Finkler et al., 2013.

	A7		▼	*fx*
	A	B	C	
1				
2	Rate	5%		
3	Periods	3		
4	Payment	(1000)		
5	PV=	(25000)		
6	$32,093.13			

Figure 8.4 Excel Example 4. *Source*: Example adapted and expanded from Finkler et al., 2013.

Readers will notice that both the payment [pmt] and *PV* values are included as negative values. This is primarily for reporting given that we always wish to report the estimated value as a positive. Hence, both of these values must be entered as negatives. Also, we did not include comma separators for monetary values in Excel. This is because commas are used to separate the different variables from one another. So if one were to include 1,000, then Excel would read this as a payment equal to one and a *PV* equal to 000.

Finally, we noted that we did not include a value for [type] in our equation. This value is included as a way to indicate to Excel whether payments are happening at the beginning or end of a year, and Excel automatically defaults to 0 assuming an end-of-the-year payment. For example, the values for this illustration would change slightly if we included a [type] value as 1 as in Figure 8.5.

The *FV* with this inclusion is equal to $32,250.75 or slightly higher since monies added at the beginning of the year have more time to compound. Hence, the school district contribution to the elementary school technology upgrade, through investing $25,000 from the school district and adding $1,000 from the elementary school for three years, which would have totaled only $28,000 if not invested, is now more than sufficient to cover the costs of the new system. Finally, it is important to note that as previously a reworking of the *FV* equation results in a useful *PV* equation that is used to compare net present costs (NPCs) as well.

Present Values with Annual Costs

Instead of having the luxury of setting aside monies for a few years to cover the costs of some new project, it is more often the case that P-12 budget managers must choose between two projects with different costs in the present.

MEDIAN						=FV(0.05, 3, -1000, -25000, 1)
	A	B	C	D	E	F
1						
2	Rate	5%				
3	Periods	3				
4	Payment	(1000)				
5	PV=	(25000)				
6	=FV(0.05, 3, -1000, -25000, 1)					
7	FV(rate, nper, pmt, [pv], [type])					

Figure 8.5   Excel Example 5. *Source*: Example adapted and expanded from Finkler et al., 2013.

P-12 budget manager are often asked to evaluate the NPC of multiple possibilities to determine which makes the most budgetary sense. To do so requires using the *PV* equation presented earlier in this chapter. Again, because this equation can become unwieldy quite quickly when including cash flows, it is presented here using Excel screenshots in a simplified version in Figures 8.6, 8.7, and 8.8.

For this example, assume that the institution has to choose between two types of computers: Computer A and Computer B. Following Finkler et al.'s (2013, p. 176) example, the information is provided in Table 8.2. From this table, it looks pretty obvious that Computer B has a higher total cost, and since most institutions seek out ways to cut costs, it might seem like a no-brainer to go with Computer A. However, this comparison is faulty. Before making a comparison, it is necessary to understand what is known about both computer options. It is clear that the initial outlay for Computer A is higher than Computer B, but the yearly costs for Computer A are substantially lower

MEDIAN	▾	× ✓ *fx*	=PV(	
	A	**B**	**C**	**D**
1		**Computer A**	**Computer B**	
2	Rate	5%	5%	
3	Periods	5	5	
4	Payment	-600	-1250	
5	**PV of Cash Flows**	=PV(		
6		PV(rate, nper, pmt, [fv], [type])		
7				
8				

Figure 8.6   Excel Example 6. *Source*: Example adapted and expanded from Finkler et al., 2013.

C13	▾		*fx*				
	A	**B**	**C**	**D**	**E**	**F**	**G**
1							
2	Rate	5%	5%	5%	5%	5%	5%
3	Payment	0	0	0	0	0	0
4	Period	0	1	2	3	4	5
5							
6		Year 0	Year 1	Year 2	Year 3	Year 4	Year 5
7	Cash In Flow	0	1200	1200	1250	1400	1475
8	Cash Out Flow	-4350	-800	-1025	-1375	-1450	-1600
9	Net Cash Flow	-4350	400	175	-125	-50	-125
10							

Figure 8.7   Excel Example 7. *Source*: Example adapted and expanded from Finkler et al., 2013.

C11		f_x	=PV(B2, C4, B3, -C9)			
	A	B	C	D	E	F	G
1							
2	Rate	5%	5%	5%	5%	5%	5%
3	Payment	0	0	0	0	0	0
4	Period	0	1	2	3	4	5
5							
6		Year 0	Year 1	Year 2	Year 3	Year 4	Year 5
7	Cash In Flow	0	1200	1200	1250	1400	1475
8	Cash Out Flow	-4350	-800	-1025	-1375	-1450	-1600
9	Net Cash Flow	-4350	400	175	-125	-50	-125
10							
11	Present Value of Individual Cash Flows	-4350	$380.95	$158.73	($107.98)	($41.14)	($97.94)
12							
13	Net Present Value	-4057.37					

Figure 8.8   Excel Example 8. *Source*: Example adapted and expanded from Finkler et al., 2013.

Table 8.2   Contrasting Computer Costs, Part 1

	Computer A	Computer B
Initial outlay	7,500	4,350
Yearly cost	600	1,250
Number of years	5	5
Total cost	**10,500**	**10,600**

than for Computer B. With this in mind, we can now employ *PV* calculations to help make the comparison appropriate.

Using the *PV* formula available in Excel, it is simple enough to carry out the calculation of multiple years of costs assuming an interest rate of 5% and five years of associated annual costs[4] and we arrive at the following:

It is necessary to calculate the *PV* of cash flows for each possible project. Again, readers will note that only the first three values are used in this instance and both [*fv*] and [type] are left out since this information is unavailable to us.

The results of these calculations are presented in Table 8.3. In this table, the cash flows for each project have been discounted. Now, it is possible to make the appropriate comparisons by adding the initial outlay to these two values to obtain the NPC of each. Hence, Computer A's NPC is equal to the initial outlay or $7,500 plus $2,597.69 or $10,097.69. For Computer B, the total NPC is equal to $4,350 plus $5,411.85 or $9,761.85. This is presented in Table 8.4.

Hence, it is clear that in discounted terms, and taking into account the yearly costs associated with each type of computer, Computer B is actually the best option based on NPC, although this analysis does not take into consideration other nonfinancial factors. The NPC analysis still provides an appropriate comparison of costs when examining options.

Table 8.3 Comparisons of Computer Cost, Part 2

	Computer A	Computer B
Rate	5%	5%
Periods	5	5
Payment	−600	−1250
PV of cash flows	**$2,597.69**	**$5,411.85**

Table 8.4 Comparisons of Computer Cost, Part 3

	Computer A	Computer B
Initial outlay	7500	4350
PV cash flows	2,597.69	5,411.85
Total NPC	**10,097.69**	**9,761.85**

NPC: Net present cost.

In this short illustration, it is our hope that readers are now familiar with the important role played by costs in the decision-making process. In the next section, we consider how projects are chosen based on situations where there are both costs and revenues associated with choosing a project that require discounting.

Net Present Value and Cash Flows

In this section, we present the foundational elements[5] associated with choosing capital projects that are associated with yearly costs and revenues. As noted by Finker et al. (2013, p. 180), the methods presented previously do not account for projects that impact both revenues and costs yearly. As this affects project valuation by requiring that the analysis account for annual cash flows, the NPV is a powerful device in the P-12 budget manager's toolkit. Now, it is important to underscore that there are at least two ways to employ this technique that allow for different values of both cash inflows and outflows for every year.

To start, let's assume that we decided to go with Computer B from the previous example. While the NPC allows us to estimate costs, it does not account for possible revenues that might accrue from choosing project B. For the sake of exposition, suppose that Computer B's system was to be used by another institution in the evenings and as a result would generate a revenue stream over the useful life of five years. Additionally, to make things a bit more interesting, we will adjust the yearly outflows, or costs, from the previous example so they are lumpier rather than the same year to year. Again, following Finkler et al. (2013, p. 181), we provide the following screenshot of the setup for calculating the NPV.

Chapter 8

	B13	▼	f_x	=SUM(B11:G11)		
	A	B	C	D	E	F	G
1							
2	Rate	5%	5%	5%	5%	5%	5%
3	Payment	0	0	0	0	0	0
4	Period	0	1	2	3	4	5
5							
6		Year 0	Year 1	Year 2	Year 3	Year 4	Year 5
7	Cash In Flow	0	1200	1200	1250	1400	1475
8	Cash Out Flow	-4350	-800	-1025	-1375	-1450	-1600
9	Net Cash Flow	-4350	400	175	-125	-50	-125
10							
11	Present Value of Individual Cash Flows	-4350	$380.95	$158.73	($107.98)	($41.14)	($97.94)
12							
13	**Net Present Value**	-4057.37					

Figure 8.9   Excel Example 9. *Source*: Example adapted and expanded from Finkler et al., 2013.

In the screen shot, the goal was to make the calculation as simple as possible using Excel's cell reference and drag functionalities. From Figure 8.7 it is clear that the rate would stay the same over every year, that the payment would be equal to zero because we are taking each year on its own, and that period is related to number of years away from the current year where the outlay is $4,350 to acquire Computer B. Once we have calculated the net cash flow for each year, discounting is required for each cash flow. This is done in the same way as before but for each year. The data reported in Figure 8.7 highlight how to go about calculating the *PV* for individual years using the cell reference function by simply dragging it across the row to obtain values for each year. If the setup is not exactly as follows, then caution must be exercised when clicking and calculating each year's *PV*.

In order to calculate the value of interest to us, the NPV, we simply tell Excel that we wish to sum all of the value in row 11 as in Figure 8.9.

As can be seen, in cell B13, which is highlighted along with the function command, we simply tell Excel that we wish to sum cells B11 through G11, which automatically adds up all of the yearly *PV*s and subtracts initial outlay to give the NPV. For decision-making, if the NPV is negative and the decision to undertake a particular course of action is purely financial, then all projects with negative NPVs should be rejected. However, if the decision is not based only on NPVs but also on other contextual factors, this comparison, like the NPC, provides valuable information about the financial portion of the decision and whether it falls short or provides a positive cash flow stream (Finkler et al., 2013).

CHOOSING THE DISCOUNT RATE

For P-12 budget managers, many decisions are analyzed based on their impact on the current budget's bottom line. Hence, there is a strong focus on choosing how to report and relate future dollars in today's monetary values. In the examples provided in this chapter, we have simply assumed that the discount rate was a given. This is problematic for fiscal administration on the whole because choosing a rate is fraught with many dilemmas.

A primary concern when accounting for the TVM is choosing a rate that best reflects the conditions facing the school district or the economy as a whole. Because the discount rate is often considered the hurdle rate, or the rate required to break even on a capital project, it must be closely tied to the school district's costs of capital (Finkler et al., 2013). Moreover, if the fiscal environment is volatile, a conservative move to deal with this uncertainty is to increase the discount rate. Still, this is extremely difficult to do well, and as a result, there are often many ways to choose the discount rate. As noted by Finkler et al. (2013, p. 185), "In practice, there is little consistency in the discount rate used across government even within branches of the same government" and the same likely holds for school districts.

Dunn (2012) provided some guidance around choosing a discount rate for public-sector entities. These include:

- Private-sector rates—These rates are based on the going interest rates in private markets with the assumption that tax monies could have been invested at these rates. The limitation with this approach is that it does not reflect external social costs and is a better indication of individual or narrow group preferences.
- Social rates—These rates are based on the social time preference related to the collective value of some cost or benefit realized into the future; it is especially concerned with the welfare of future generations. It attempts to overcome the short-term emphasis often placed on TVM analysis. Still, it is often accused of being inefficient because it is lower than private rates.
- Government rates—These rates are based on the current costs of borrowing faced by governments. The difficulty in using this rate is that different levels of government often borrow at different rates. Additionally, it does not account for the opportunity cost associated when monies are not invested (pp. 232–33).

As we hope is evident, each one of these alternatives has both advantages and limitations. In any event, the goal should be to incorporate as much information about the fiscal environment as possible as P-12 budget managers undertake the analysis of investments in capital projects and their true costs.

Finally, there exists some concern around choosing a discount rate while accounting for inflationary pressures. A preferred approach is to forecast anticipated inflationary pressures on inflows and outflows before calculating the *PV* and *FV* of each. Another approach is to include the anticipated inflation rate in the discount rate. The limitation introduced with this approach is that it does not account for differences in the impacts of inflationary pressures on different inflows or outflows.

CONCLUSION

The content of this chapter was designed to provide a basic overview of the capital budgeting process and cycle. It has included a basic introduction to the importance of the TVM and its related concepts such as FV, PV, annuities, NPC, and NPV. Additionally, it has provided guidance regarding choosing projects and a discount rate in the capital budgeting process. While the emphasis in this chapter has been on capital budgeting without debt, the same concepts apply to the capital budgeting cycle and process with debt. In the next section, we examine this further.

GUIDING QUESTIONS

The following questions address many of the key concepts covered in chapter 8. Readers should be able to answer these questions upon completion of the chapter:

1. How does capital budgeting differ from operational budgeting?
2. What are the major approaches to capital budgeting when trying to avoid the use of debt?
3. How is capital budgeting related to operational budgeting?
4. Why does there exist a need to take into consideration how money changes value over time? How does this relate to fiscal administration and budgeting decisions?

ADDITIONAL READING

Those readers desiring additional information on the concepts addressed in chapter 8 should consult the following:

Brimley, Jr., V., D. A. Verstegen, & R. R. Garfield. 2012. *Financing education in a climate of change* (11th ed.). Boston, MA: Pearson. (Pay particular attention to chapter 11.)

Earthman, G. I. 2009. *Planning educational facilities: What educators need to know* (3rd ed.). New York: Rowman & Littlefield Education. (Pay particular attention to chapter 7.)

EXERCISES

The following exercises are designed to provide readers the opportunity to take the concepts addressed in chapter 8 and apply them using actual data.

1. Using the following vignettes, employ the *discounting* techniques presented in this chapter:
   a. Assume that the school district has a capital asset that will be worth $99,523.03 in 5 years and that the discount rate for this time period is 3%. Provide the present value of this capital asset. What happens to the value of this asset if the discount rate changes to 5%? Compare how the change in discount rates affects the assumed value of the asset.
   b. Assume that the school district has a capital asset that will be worth $93,862.47 in 10 years and that the discount rate for this time period is 3%. Provide the present value of this capital asset. What happens to the value of this asset if the discount rate changes to 3.5%? Compare how the change in discount rates affects the assumed value of the asset.
   c. Assume that the school district has a capital asset that will be worth $120,844 in 20 years and that the discount rate for this time period is 3%. Provide the present value of this capital asset. What happens if the discount rate changes to 4%? Compare how the change in discount rates affects the assumed value of the asset.
2. What happens to the confidence of the estimated value of our asset as we go further into the future assuming a particular discount rate?
3. After completing the previous three exercises, comment on how accurate each is likely to be based on the specifics of each problem. Is a 5-, 10-, or 20-year forecast more accurate? Explain why each is or is not more accurate? What should a P-12 budget manager consider when calculating *PV*s using a 20-year period?
4. Which factors should be included when choosing a discount rate? How should capital budgeting incorporate inflationary concerns?
   Using the following vignettes, employ the *compounding* techniques presented in this chapter:

a. Assume that a school district will invest $117,315.40 for 5 years and that the discount rate for this time period is 5%. Provide the future value of this investment. What happens to the value of this investment if the interest (discount) rate changes to 3%? Compare how the change in rates affects the assumed value of the investment.

b. Assume that a school district will invest $109,633.30 for 10 years and that the discount rate for this time period is 5%. Provide the future value of this investment. What happens to the value of this investment if the interest rate changes to 3%? Compare how the change in rates affects the assumed value of the investment.

c. Assume that a school district will invest $95,876.21 for 20 years and that the discount rate for this time period is 5%. Provide the future value of this investment. What happens to the value of this investment if the interest rate changes to 3%? Compare how the change in rates affects the assumed value of the investment.

d. Using the information from Exercise c, reexamine this problem, but this time assume that compounding happens twice a year. Compare the differences in the investment value at 5% and at 3% to those calculated in Exercise c. How does this change the calculation? What happens to the value of an investment when compound periods are increased to more than once a year?

5. Using the information provided, as well as Microsoft Excel, apply the ideas presented around *cash flows and decision-making* to answer the following questions:

     A school district must choose between providing an art exhibition space with the following outlays and cash flows. Using examples provided in this chapter, calculate the NPC for each project and explain which exhibition space should be chosen based solely on the NPC.

6. Briefly describe how the process would be different for calculating the NPC if the cash flows differed from time period to time period?

7. Should the NPC be the most important or only determinant for choosing a project? If so, why? If not, what others things might be included?

	Exhibition A	Exhibition B
Initial outlay	$10,500	$6,350
Yearly cost	−500	−1200
Periods (years)	5	5
Interest rate	4.5%	4.5%
Total cost	**$13,000**	**$12,350**

NOTES

1. For ease of analysis, in the instance, periods are understood as years because the market rate of interest is assumed to be paid annually. However, this can change even for compounding periods presented in this chapter.

2. Based on the *PV* example presented earlier, it is clear that the institution needs to invest about $21,596 today at 5% to receive $25,000 in three years.

3. If the *FV* is already known, another possibility is to discount the *FV* by the increased number of periods and lower rate when interest is paid more than once a year to obtain the needed amount for investment today or the *PV*.

4. It is possible to assume that yearly payments are not equal over time; however, that is beyond the scope of the current text (see Finkler et al., 2013).

5. For detailed explanation and treatment of valuation, cash flow, and discount models, see Damodaran (2001, 2012).

Chapter 9

Capital Budgeting and Debt

School and school district officials often face capital budgeting choices that require more funds than available either in reserves or as surpluses to the total program. This requires school district officials to carry debt in the form of bonds, typically, to complete these types of expensive capital projects. To help those individuals new to the post of P-12 budget manager, a brief introduction and overview to capital budgeting as related to issuing and using debt as a financing tool is provided in this chapter.

As the foundations of fiscal analysis regarding the time value of money do not change for the issuance of bonds, the fundamentals covered in chapter 8 remain largely unchanged for capital budgeting with this type of debt and, hence, are not covered here. Also, the intricacies of bond issuance and debt management are beyond the scope of the current text; however, those wishing to obtain a more nuanced and accessible understanding of the process should refer to the references at the end of the chapter.

WHAT IS BONDING?

Bonding is a tool available to school district officials to secure significant amounts of equity for major capital projects, such as new construction or renovation of existing facilities. Each year school district officials receive public funds from a combination of local, state, and federal taxes. These public dollars make up the school district's total program, or its annual budget. However, a school district's total program does not include sufficient resources for major facility construction or renovation projects.

In order for school district officials to obtain the required resources to fund a capital project, they must successfully encourage voters within the school district's boundaries to approve a bond. The bond, in essence, is a promissory note that acts like a mortgage for the school district. The duration of the bond is specified in the ballot initiative that voters decide on. Most bonds in public education last for 20–30 years. Once approved, the school district receives the total amount of money from a financial institution, and they can begin the capital projects. The payment on the bond is derived from additional mills being levied on all property owners within the school district.

WHY USE DEBT?

Generally speaking, school district officials and, ultimately, school boards will issue debt in the form of bonds to finance large capital projects. Examples of these projects include the construction, refurbishment, or renovation of schools and administrative buildings (Earthman, 2009). Additionally, and as noted in chapter 8, the capital budgeting process takes place over a number of years and is decidedly related to the long-term goals of the school district (Barr & McClellan, 2011a, b; Goldstein, 2012).

As a result, projects requiring debt financing should include both long-term and short-term considerations since servicing this debt typically requires long-standing dedication of financial resources both in the form of debt service and operating and maintenance expenses. Moreover, although some of the financing methods mentioned previously, such as pay-as-you-go (Paygo) and capital campaigns, offer the prospect of funding capital projects without debt or interest costs (Lee, Johnson, & Joyce, 2013), given the scope of most capital projects for public school districts these types of options are not typically viable.

Therefore, issuing bonds to finance a capital project allows school district officials to fund projects that would be outside the school district's total program. Bonding allows the school district to acquire capital assets that should help it fulfill its mission, goals, and vision by using debt to create safe learning environments for students or purchase land without putting undue strain on total program.

In addition, bonding allows the school district to spread the costs of a large capital acquisition or project over a much longer period of time. Debt service and depreciation of capital assets are spread over the useful life of a project. This means that the school district reports only the depreciation and debt-service for the current fiscal year.

CREDIT RATINGS AND FACTORS RELATED TO BOND RATES[1]

In determining how much a school district will pay for debt, credit ratings agencies consider a number of factors. This rating offers information for those who purchase bonds and provides a means of establishing default risk associated with a specific school district. Given the fact that the revenues required to pay the bond are derived from property taxes, a school district bond is typically viewed as a secure investment. The specific factors that credit rating agencies use to rate school districts are discussed in the sections that follow.

Credit Rating Symbols and Qualifiers

Credit ratings of school districts consist of various summative symbols to assess the potential risk for investors. These symbols are detailed in Table 9.1. A quick note: Table 9.1 includes only those ratings issued by Standard & Poor's (S&P) and Moody's given their long history rating colleges and universities.[2]

Generally speaking, school districts enjoy relatively high, stable credit ratings. However, this trend has changed recently with downgrades becoming more commonplace (Bogaty & Nelson, 2013; Daley, 2010; S&P, 2013) due primarily to the economic downturn of 2008. When viewed in aggregate, the sector remains rather stable, though S&P (2013) noted that downgrades as compared to upgrades were increasing since 2008.

While the news from S&P is somewhat more positive than Moody's in terms of its general outlook for the sector, both agencies remain tentative regarding possible changes impacting credit ratings in P-12 public education. While the vast majority of school districts are seen as creditworthy, increasing levels of deferred maintenance and competitive pressures will undoubtedly require capital financing.

Table 9.1 Credit Ratings for School Districts

	S&P	*Moody's*	
Highest rating	AAA	Aaa	Highest rating
	AA	Aa	
	A	A	
	BBB	Baa	
Speculative	BB	Ba	Speculative
	B	B	
	CCC	Caa	
	CC	Ca	
	C	C	In default/lowest rating
In default/ lowest rating*	D	N/A	
Qualifiers	Plus and minus indicate a relatively stronger or weaker position in the category	1 indicates a higher, 2 a median, and 3 a lower position in the category	

Sources: Serna (2013a, b), reproduced with permission.
*Note that in the case of the default credit rating S&P maintains one rating more than does Moody's.

It will be interesting to watch rating trends in the future as more capital projects that are funded with bond dollars include general upkeep efforts that have historically been funded with total program dollars. For example, historically, school district officials would use capital funds from the total program to replace a roof on a high school. However, current trends suggest these types of projects are being rolled into bonding efforts, which means the property owners are being asked to pay for the cost of the upkeep project along with the interest. It is possible that the more money school districts bond for will result in lower credit ratings.

In bond markets, a school district's credit rating determines how much it will pay in interest for this debt over the duration of the loan. The expenses associated with issuing bonds are directly related to the creditworthiness of the issuing entity. In other words, even for school districts within the same category, the costs associated with bond issuance can vary considerably based on differing qualifiers.

Ratings, Debt Service, and the Total Program

The fact that ratings, and the accompanying qualifiers, determine interest costs on bond issues results in at least a few important considerations for P-12 budget managers. First, operating budgets must be able to accommodate debt-service and depreciation costs as well as those concomitant expenses required to bring and keep a project online.

Second, bond issues impact a school district's debt profile and total debt-burden. To be clear, school districts with excessive debt will see a drop in their overall credit rating. Credit becomes unavailable for other projects when school district officials pass a bond for specified projects. This will impact long-run fiscal positioning because the pledge of operating revenues means that these funds cannot be pledged for other projects. Moreover, this could signal to debt markets that the school district has overleveraged its assets.

Third, in the process of making decisions about the uses of limited resources, changes in a school district's credit rating could indicate that decision-makers are not making the best trade-offs as far as debt markets are concerned. Indeed, a major part of the ratings process is related to how school district officials are managing debt now and did so in the past. Furthermore, rating agencies carefully examine current and previous debt-management and debt-service policies (Serna, 2013a, b).

Associated Rating Factors

Evaluating the creditworthiness of school districts is fraught with many complexities. Rating agencies evaluate a vast array of local, state, and financial characteristics. Mostly, the agencies wish to establish the school district's demand and market-positioning, finances and operating performance, internal and external management and governance. Also considered are the school district's debt profile, state policies, and statutes.

The general credit rating criteria, including some examples of how each category is evaluated, are outlined in Table 9.2. Based on the demands placed on school districts for determining creditworthiness, the data contained in a rating serve as important indicators for P-12 budget managers, debt markets, and external stakeholders related to the fiscal health of the school district. The rating supplies information on short- and long-term fiscal stability of an institution. As a result, these ratings often provide invaluable information and guidance for future strategic endeavors both internally and externally.

The discussion on school district credit ratings has resulted in a preview into what is generally a multifaceted practice. However, it is clear that the rating agencies evaluate school districts based on a multitude of factors.

Finally, credit rating agencies have stated that a number of the factors they consider when rating school districts are difficult to quantify. Still, the highly contextual operational environment facing each school district remains exceedingly important for determining its credit rating and, by extension, debt costs. In order to understand the complexity of the process a bit better, the next section looks at how school districts go about issuing debt and the actors in the process.

Table 9.2 General Public School District Credit Rating Criteria

Criterion	Measurement Indicators
Market position and demand	Net assessed value (NAV) of the school district—the value of a mill in a school district is determined by the NAV. Higher NAVs result in a lower number of mills required to obtain the local contribution to the school district's total program
Finances and operating performance	Revenues, expenses, risk management, operating budgets and balance sheets, endowment and long-term investment pools, liquidity provisions, and total debt burden
Governance and management	Overall school district strategies and policies implemented by central office administration, track record of dealing with unforeseen difficulties, tenure of management, and composition and structure of the school board, reporting mechanisms, and monitoring procedures
Debt profile	Security pledges, debt covenants, as well as other liabilities and debt instruments
State policies and government relationship	State-imposed limits on indebtedness, state limits on the total value of mill levy overrides, and the make up (political leaning) of the state board of education

Sources: Serna (2013a, b), reproduced with permission.

ACTORS IN THE BOND PROCESS AND
STEPS FOR ISSUING DEBT

As can be inferred from the previous section, issuing debt is complicated. To help illuminate some of the components of a debt issue, a concise introduction to the process including some of the major actors is provided in this section. It then outlines the major steps associated with a bond issue that relate directly to higher education. Again, the goal here is to provide a 35,000-foot view of the process. Those seeking a more nuanced understanding should consult the references at the end of the chapter.

Actors in a Bond Issue

In most bond issues, actors can be broken up into three categories: the issuers, the bond dealers, and the investors. Each of these actors is discussed here:

Issuers—The issuers in this instance are school districts and, more accurately, the voters in the school district boundaries once the bond is passed (Ely, 2012). Additionally, public school districts may have access to a statewide credit enhancement programs that serves as an alternative to traditional, private bond insurance (Ely, 2012).

Bond dealers—This group usually includes financial planners, bankers, public finance specialists, underwriters, traders, sales, research, and credit analysts, operations, and bond counsel. Public finance specialists, who are investment bankers, serve as the point of contact for issuers and underwriters. They provide guidance for the sale and selection of an underwriter. Underwriters then purchase bonds and as a result set both the interest rates and prices on the issue. Traders are individuals in the secondary market that trade bonds among other dealers and investors.

Sales includes those who are responsible for maintaining relationships with either individual or institutional investors such as mutual, pension, or hedge funds and banks. Research and credit analysts are charged with monitoring and reviewing issuers. In addition, there are operational responsibilities when a bond is issued. Operations refer to all of the record-keeping, order-processing, and payments related to a bond. Finally, bond counsel includes lawyers that represent the legal interests of bondholders, underwriters, and issuers.

Once more, the simple number of actors included in a bond issue is significant. And this is to say nothing of rating agencies, special financial consultants, bond brokers, bond insurers, and banks, all of whom add to the number of actors and complexity of the process. This should, again, highlight the need for prudence when deciding on a bond issue. Issuing debt is an expensive and time-consuming proposition and, therefore, should not be taken lightly.

Investors—Investors are individuals, households, or institutional entities. They are the final owners of the bond debt—the bondholders. As noted by O'Hara (2012, p. 18), "The principal characteristic of all buyers of traditional municipal securities [education bonds] is that they are subject to federal income tax so that they benefit from the tax exemption." In other words, investors often choose this vehicle because interest income is frequently exempt from both federal and state/local taxes. This is a benefit for education because it is this characteristic of their debt that makes it especially attractive to investors.

Finally, to help round out the discussion about issuing debt, the next section introduces readers to the stepwise process associated with a bond issue. The goal of doing so is to provide individuals who are new to fiscal administration not just with a descriptive account of who is involved, but also to familiarize them with the actual process itself.

Steps in a Bond Issue

The objective of this section is to provide novice P-12 budget managers with a working understanding of the bond issue process. As noted previously, the aim of this chapter is to provide information for those who find themselves with little budgetary administration experience, but who, nonetheless, must make decisions around capital acquisitions and the process of using debt to fund capital projects.

Following both O'Hara (2012) and Weyl and Rodgers (2006, pp. 2–3) in summative fashion, the stepwise process as a whole and a short description of each step are given in Table 9.3. Readers will note that many of the components of a bond issue reflect the capital budgeting process as outlined in chapter 8. The 12 steps discussed in Table 9.3 are presented in sequential order.

The information presented in Table 9.3 has provided an overview for the typical school district bond cycle. As new P-12 budget managers engage in the process of resource allocation, it is important to become a savvy consumer of information that relates to long-term financial planning. Becoming knowledgeable about debt and institutional requirements for issuing bonds is a first step in this process.

CONCLUSION

Admittedly, this chapter has provided a concise overview of capital budgeting with regard to debt. However, this information should provide a solid

Table 9.3   Stepwise Process for a Bond Issue

Step in Bond Issue	Description
Clearly establish the use of bond proceeds	In this step, the goal is to determine if new projects will be financed through a bond
Obtain approvals	School district officials should seek and obtain approval from the local school board
Choose a bond dealer	Often entails employing a securities firm or bank; care should be taken because this entity sets the requirements regarding process and time frame. The bank will typically provide assistance with the bond campaign
Craft a working group	Choose professionals in the community who will work on the bond issue. This group will develop grassroots support for the bond throughout the community
Develop timeline	A timeline for bond issues is typically a two-year process
Engage credit agencies	School districts should seek a rating from at least one, often two, rating agencies
Generate and review documents	Bond issues are labor and paperwork intensive processes, and this step should focus on gathering, generating, and reviewing all necessary documents that will demonstrate the school district's need
Conduct a tax analysis	Examine pre- and postissue tax consequences and requirements, including the use of projects funded by tax-exempt bonds, capital campaign restrictions, and bond proceed investment
Hold the election*	A bond initiative must be approved by a majority of voters in order for the bond to be authorized
Close the issue	Sign all documents, verify that all reports and documents are included, and make sure that bond proceeds are delivered to the bond trustee
Disburse proceeds	This process usually happens over time; proceeds are distributed based on wording of the approved bond and an established timeline
Deal with postclosing	School district officials are required to follow rules around investment of bond funds, disclosures, and compliance

*Note that a bond election is not required in all states.

foundation to begin understanding the role of debt and credit ratings in the fiscal administration of school districts. In closing, a major takeaway from this chapter should be that issuing debt in the form of bonds, or even other long-term debt vehicles, is certainly a decision that school district officials should not take lightly.

When deciding whether to issue bonds, school district officials should carefully weigh the short- and long-term effects of such a decision. As decisions around debt are made, special attention should be focused not only on the total amount of debt, its related service, and depreciation, but also on the impacts that new projects, building, and acquisitions will have on the operating position of the school district.

GUIDING QUESTIONS

The following questions address many of the key concepts covered in chapter 9. Readers should be able to answer these questions upon completion of the chapter:

1. How do bonds differ from mill levy overrides?
2. What are the purposes of bonds?
3. How much debt is acceptable for public school districts?
4. What factors positively and negatively impact a school district's credit rating?
5. How does a school district's credit rating impact future bonding efforts?

ADDITIONAL READING

Those readers desiring additional information on the concepts addressed in chapter 9 should consult the following:

Brimley, Jr., V., D. A. Verstegen, & R. R. Garfield. 2012. *Financing education in a climate of change* (11th ed.). Boston, MA: Pearson. (Pay particular attention to chapter 11.)

Earthman, G. I. 2009 *Planning educational facilities: What educators need to know* (3rd ed.). New York: Rowman & Littlefield Education. (Pay particular attention to chapter 7.)

EXERCISES

The following exercises are designed to provide readers the opportunity to take the concepts addressed in chapter 9 and apply them using actual data.

1. A school district levies 22.222 mills to generate sufficient funds for the local contribution to the total program. In this state, only 7.96% of a residential property is taxed (this is the case in Colorado). How much would an individual residential property owner of a home worth $300,000 pay in taxes to support the local school district?
2. If the same school district had a net assessed value of $4,100,481,000, and it successfully passed a bond for $200,000,000 for 20 years, which produced an annual bond payment of $5,155,247.85, and residential properties amounted to 46% of the net assessed value, how much more would the home owner in question 1 pay as a result of the passed bond?

3. Identify potential dangers with rolling capital outlay projects, such as basic upkeep of a school building, into a bond.

NOTES

1. Portions of this section are adapted, with permission, from Serna (2013a, b).

2. A third rating agency is Fitch's, which is not included here because its history with rating institutions of higher education is relatively short as compared to S&P's and Moody's. Additionally, Fitch's rating criteria are analogous to those provided by S&P and Moody's.

Phase IV

LINKAGE, PHILOSOPHY, AND CONCLUSION

The focus of the final phase is alignment. The aspiring P-12 budget manager must realize that spending decisions should align with the organization's mission, vision, goals, and strategic plan. In addition, aspiring P-12 budget managers must recognize the repercussions if spending patterns do not align with the stated values of the organization. Moreover, P-12 budget managers are encouraged to develop their own philosophy related to managing public funds. The practice of writing down a philosophy is essential and this philosophy statement can serve as a tool to guide budget-related decisions.

Chapter 10

Budget Alignment with Strategic Plan

There is a saying related to budgets that holds a multitude of implications for those charged with overseeing P-12 funds. "Don't tell me what you value, show me your budget and I will tell you what you value." P-12 budget managers should be cognizant of the fact that spending patterns directly influence and, in some situations, even determine the values of a school or a school district. Ultimately, all within a school district charged with managing and overseeing budgets need guiding principles that can ensure that spending patterns are establishing the desired values and norms within the organization. The purpose of this chapter is to identify where these guiding principles can be found and how P-12 budget managers can use the guiding principles to the betterment of the entire organization.

GUIDING PRINCIPLES WITHIN AN ORGANIZATION

In general there are four documents within any organization that P-12 budget managers should use as guiding principles when monitoring spending patterns. These are:

1. Mission Statement: According to Yukl (2002, p. 284), a "mission statement usually describes the purpose of the organization in terms of the type of activities to be performed." A mission statement describes what an organization is attempting to do in the present. Consider the following school district mission statement, "Educate . . . every child, every day" (Poudre School District, n.d.)—what trends would you expect to see when analyzing this school district's spending patterns? Ideally, the

expenditures should document the organization's commitment to educating every child every day.

2. Vision Statement: Whereas a mission statement's focus is the present, a vision statement provides people within an organization a view of what the school or school district is striving to become in the future. The vision statement provides a vision for the future and, when properly written, elicits excitement and stimulates individuals to apply their energy and creativity toward the end goal (Yukl, 2002, p. 284). An example of a vision statement could be, "Our school district will become a school district of excellence by promoting rigor, relevance, relationships, responsibilities, and results." The immediate spending patterns should allocate funds in a way that promotes rigor, relevance, relationships, responsibilities, and results. Proposed expenditures that failed to align with the desired attributes should not be approved.

3. Goals: Goals within a P-12 organization relate directly to the mission and vision statements. Educational leaders will collaboratively develop both short- and long-term goals for the school or school district to ensure that daily actions align with the vision (Fink & Markholt, 2011, p. 172). The long- and short-terms goals serve as a reminder that the daily actions within an organization should direct the school or school district toward the mission and vision statements.

4. Strategic Plan: The strategic plan serves to move a school or a school district from where it is today closer toward its vision statement over a finite amount of time. A strategic plan helps "school administrators turn visionary goals into reality" (Whitehead, Boschee, & Decker, 2013, pp. 100–101). The aim of a strategic plan is to identify specific actions that will be taken within an organization over a predetermined amount of time (typically, strategic plans work in five-year increments). These specific actions, if achieved, should help move the school or the school district closer to its vision statement and goals.

Although each of these documents is unique and serves a specific purpose, taken together they provide a P-12 budget manager with a tool to gauge the appropriateness of any and all proposed expenditures. Ultimately, each expenditure request should align with the four documents discussed earlier or, in general, it should not be approved.

MISALIGNMENT EXAMPLES

The potential for misalignment between the mission, vision, goals, and strategic plan of a school or school district and the actual spending patterns is great.

What follows are a number of examples of how spending patterns misalign with the mission, vision, goals, and strategic plan. However, before these examples are discussed, a pivotal question must be asked and answered. Why is misalignment a potential problem?

The danger with misalignment is that poor spending decisions fail to enable a school or school district to improve and better serve students. If school or school district officials are approving proposed expenditures that do not align with the organization's mission, vision, goals, and strategic plan, then the organization is more likely to remain mired in the status quo. For example, consider the dieter who accepts every free sample at the grocery store and then cannot figure out why the diet is not working. Or the person who wants to put a small amount of money away for the eventual retirement every month but fails to do so because those dollars are being spent on entertainment.

Failure to align spending patterns with the organization's mission, vision, goals, and strategic plan is akin to these two examples. The organization will fail to move ahead and improve. In other words, educational leaders focused on improving a school or school district cannot afford to allow misalignment to occur.

Misalignment Example #1

Ms. Scott is a principal of a high school in Texas. The vision statement for the school, developed three years ago, reads, "Educational excellence for all." At the start of the current school year, the school's budget included an allotment of $20,000 for each department. Ms. Scott worked with the building leadership team to develop the following allocation of the department funds:

Table 10.1 Department Allocations

Department	Budget Allocation ($)
Athletics	5,000
Counseling	500
Drivers' education	1,000
Family and consumer sciences	100
Foreign language	350
Language arts	1,250
Mathematics	1,000
Music	3,000
Physical education	5,000
Science	1,700
Social studies	900
Special education	200
Total allocation	20,000

The building leadership team consists of Ms. Scott, the two assistant principals, and 10 department heads. Everyone on the building leadership team approved the budget allocation.

Here are some guiding questions to consider when analyzing this example:

- What does the budget allocation say about the vision of the school?
- Does that vision align with the school's stated vision?
- What would the budget allocation look like if it were to better align with the school's stated vision statement?

Misalignment Example #2

Mike Holmes is the newly appointed principal of Spark Elementary School. After reviewing the school's improvement plan, student achievement data, and exit survey data from teachers, Mike concludes there are two pressing issues at the school: the need for a focused student intervention program and attention on faculty morale. Mike came from a school that had successfully implemented a multitiered system of support (MTSS) that simultaneously reduced behavior referrals and increased student achievement. He really wants to allocate $5,000 from the Spark Elementary School budget toward training teachers on MTSS.

Mike also noticed that in the exit survey from the previous school year, the overall teacher morale was at an all-time low for the school. The $5,000 could be spent in a way that would address the morale issue, but Mike does not feel like he could do both with the limited funds with any degree of fidelity. He knows that his job performance, ultimately, will be based on student achievement, so he wants to spend the money on the MTSS training and implementation.

Table 10.2

Department	Budget Allocation ($)
Athletics	
Counseling	
Drivers' education	
Family and consumer sciences	
Foreign language	
Language arts	
Mathematics	
Music	
Physical education	
Science	
Social studies	
Special education	
Total allocation	20,000

One line from the school's goals jumps out at Mike—The faculty and staff at Spark Elementary School will work to create a healthy and happy workplace. However, Mike decides to spend the money on the MTSS training as opposed to addressing the teacher morale concerns. Did he make the right decision?

Final Thoughts Related to Misalignment

Too often P-12 budget managers fall into the trap of either-or thinking and fail to use creative problem-solving skills to maximize the potential of limited public dollars. The either-or way of thinking can be defined as only seeing two options—either this or that—and nothing else. For example, in the second misalignment example, Mike, the principal, should not feel like he needs to choose between the MTSS training and addressing faculty morale. Rather, he should seek additional funding to make both necessities a reality at the school. The additional funding could be obtained from the school district, the parent-teacher organization, or the community in the form of gifts, grants, or donations.

Either-or thinking will harm a school or school district. Educational leaders charged with managing and overseeing budgets cannot afford to think either-or. Instead, leaders need to get in the habit of supporting creative, and costly, ideas by reducing barriers and identifying alternative solutions. Recently, a Colorado superintendent asked all of the administrators in the school district to "Make yes a habit." That slogan captures the alternative of either-or thinking and succinctly reminds educational leaders to support others by eliminating barriers to improvement.

In analyzing the two misalignment examples, it should be stressed that all four options—allocating department funds toward athletics or allocating funds toward academics; training staff members on MTSS or addressing faculty morale issues—are legitimate proposed expenditures. That is why a P-12 budget manager must use the mission, vision, goals, and strategic plan to guide decisions around fiscal allocations. Using the idea that there are good decisions, better decisions, and best decisions for a school or a school district, P-12 budget managers should strive to always make the best financial decisions. Ultimately, the best decisions occur when the spending patterns align with the organization's mission, vision, goals, and strategic plan.

REVISITING MISSION, VISION, GOALS, AND STRATEGIC PLAN

How often should leaders within a school or school district revisit the organization's mission, vision, goals, and strategic plan? Unfortunately, there is not a set answer to that question for every school or school district. However, implicit in the question is the idea that educational leaders should regularly revisit each of the documents that are guiding the spending patterns of a school or a school district. The thought of using a mission statement that is over 20 years old to guide current spending decisions seems misguided, assuming the mission statement no longer reflects the current direction of the organization.

It should be noted that revisiting the mission, vision, goals, and strategic plan does not necessarily mean that these documents are going to be rewritten regularly. Instead, revisiting suggests that educational leaders will review the current mission, vision, goals, and strategic plan for the organization on a regular basis to ensure that these statements continue to reflect the current needs of the school or school district.

School districts and schools are accredited by either state and/or regional organizations. These accreditation visits typically occur every seven to ten years and would serve as an opportunity to regularly revisit the organization's mission, vision, goals, and strategic plan. In addition, as leaders prepare for accreditation visits, those within the organization can be invited to collaboratively participate in this process to ensure that each of the documents truly reflects the collective and shared aspirations for the school or school district.

ANALYZING SPENDING PATTERNS

The role of analyzing spending patterns within an organization is paramount for P-12 budget managers. The analysis of spending patterns could also be referred to as auditing current practices, a concept that was discussed in detail in chapter 7. However, audits can focus on different aspects related to spending patterns. At the most basic level, an audit ensures there are sufficient funds in each of the accounts for the approved expenditures. In addition, audits are conducted to ensure that those entrusted with overseeing P-12 budgets are adhering to school district policy and generally accepted accounting requirements.

Specific to this discussion, there is another type of audit that P-12 budget managers can conduct that will encourage that all spending decisions align with the mission, vision, goals, and strategic plan of the school or school district. This type of audit of spending patterns would examine the stated mission, vision, goals, and strategic plan of the organization and the actual allocations and then offer an assessment on how well the two actually align.

This type of audit does not necessarily occur regularly in schools or school districts, but if educational leaders genuinely want the stated mission, vision, goals, and strategic plan to guide the organization's improvement process, then such an audit must occur at least annually. It is only when leaders ask other leaders how a particular spending decision aligns with the stated mission, vision, goals, and strategic plan that behaviors will change for the better.

Status quo is the enemy to improvement, and too many schools and school districts are mired in doing the same thing as they have always done because leaders are failing to fully grasp the power of budgets in bringing about change. Money drives everything that is done in public education, and educational leaders who ensure spending decisions align with the school or school district's mission, vision, goals, and strategic plan are maximizing the potential of each dollar to improve the organization.

CORRECTING SPENDING PATTERNS

The next question that needs to be explored is what should be done if spending decisions fail to align with the school or school district's mission, vision, goals, and strategic plan? Two specific strategies will be discussed—one focused on an individual educator who might struggle with alignment and one aimed at altering the culture and climate of the organization.

Inevitably, there will be a handful of educators that will struggle with grasping the importance of ensuring spending decisions align with the organization's mission, vision, goals, and strategic plan. Leaders working with such educators should take the time to meet with these individuals and explain why alignment is essential. Effective leaders will initiate this conversation before making a decision on the proposed expenditure. For example, it would make sense to ask a teacher to explain how the proposed expenditure aligns with the mission, vision, goals, and strategic plan. If the educator is unable to do so, then invite her or him to come back with a concrete answer.

A sound practice to help an entire organization appreciate the importance of alignment would be to require the educator initiating the purchase order to identify, on the actual purchase order form, how the proposed expenditure supports the mission, vision, goals, and strategic plan of the organization. This practice will encourage all who are initiating purchase orders to become more familiar with the school or school district's mission, vision, goals, and strategic plan. In addition, purchase order forms that require educators to address alignment will serve as a filter to eliminate frivolous expenditure proposals.

CONCLUSION

All educators, including educational leaders charged with overseeing and managing budgets, should recognize the importance of alignment between spending patterns and the organization's mission, vision, goals, and strategic plan. In short, alignment enables an organization to improve whereas misalignment condemns an organization to remain mired in status quo. A lot of time should be put into the development of the mission, vision, goals, and strategic plan, and these documents, when properly created and implemented into an organization, should collectively identify the desired direction for becoming better. By encouraging alignment of spending decisions to the mission, vision, goals, and strategic plan, P-12 budget managers will maximize the value of each dollar within the budget and support the school or school district in the improvement process.

GUIDING QUESTIONS

The following questions address many of the key concepts covered in chapter 10. Readers should be able to answer these questions upon completion of the chapter:

1. How do mission statements, vision statements, goals, and strategic plan help P-12 budget managers know where to allocate the resources for a school district?
2. What should a P-12 budget manager do if spending patterns do not align with the school district's mission statement, vision statement, goals, and/or strategic plan?

ADDITIONAL READING

For the readers that would like additional information on the topics addressed in chapter 10, we offer the following recommendations:

Garner, C. W. 2004. *Education finance for school leaders.* Upper Saddle River, NJ: Pearson. (Pay attention to chapter 5.)
Odden, A. R., & L. O. Picus. 2014. *School finance: A policy perspective* (5th ed.). New York, NY: McGraw Hill. (Pay attention to chapter 8.)

EXERCISES

The following exercises are designed to provide readers the opportunity to take the concepts addressed in chapter 10 and apply them using actual data.

1. Access the mission statement, vision statement, goals, and strategic plan of a particular school district.
2. Review each of those documents.
3. Access the most current budget from the same school district.

Once steps 1–3 are complete, answer the following questions:

1. What are the stated values of the school district based on the mission statement, vision statement, goals, and strategic plan?
2. What are the observable values of the school district based on the spending patterns reported in the budget report?
3. What do the spending patterns say about the values of the school district?
4. How well do the values and spending decisions align?

Chapter 11

Conclusion

At the beginning of this book we introduced the idea that money is central to all that is done in public education. Then, in an effort to better illustrate the importance of proper fiscal management, we divided the discussion embedded throughout this book into four different phases. The focus of the first phase was the foundational knowledge a budget manager needs in order to effectively oversee public funds and maximize the educational opportunities of all students. Some of the pertinent topics covered in the first phase included revenues, expenditures, financial ratios, and forecasting.

In the second phase, we shifted the discussion to address the steps that P-12 budget managers should take when developing and overseeing budgets. We reviewed the typical budget cycle for a P-12 budget manager. Then, we reviewed concepts related to overseeing and auditing P-12 budgets. We also analyzed the concept of variance analysis.

For the third phase, our discussion centered on capital budgeting. Specifically, we reviewed strategies that P-12 budget managers and administrators can consider when attempting to fund capital projects either with or without debt. The aim of the fourth and final phase was to help aspiring and practicing P-12 budget managers develop their own philosophy related to managing a public school budget and appreciate the importance of aligning spending practices to the organization's vision, mission, goals, and strategic plan.

In addition to the discussion provided throughout the book, we have attempted to provide the reader with practical examples that took the different theoretical concepts and applied them to "real-life" situations. These practical examples were, ultimately, the reason we wrote this book. We knew there were plenty of outstanding school finance and budgeting textbooks available. What we felt was missing for aspiring P-12 budget managers was an opportunity to apply the budgetary concepts into practice. We recognize the importance of experience in the learning process, and it is our hope that the experiences provided to readers through the various exercises in this book have solidified their understanding of budgeting practices.

In conclusion, we would like to review those overarching concepts that we hope every reader gained a better understanding of and appreciation for as a result of this book.

KNOW WHO TO ASK

As we have stated throughout this book, we recognize that most aspiring educational leaders pursue leadership positions due to their commitment and expertise in areas such as curriculum or leadership. Very few seek leadership positions as a result of their budgetary abilities. However, it is essential for all leaders to become experts in managing budgets.

It is our contention that this book will lay a basic foundation that will enable aspiring P-12 leaders to, eventually, become experts in managing budgets. However, the suave leaders will continue to seek out opportunities to grow in their abilities to manage a P-12 budget. Part of growing as a budget manager includes dialoguing with others that possess greater expertise. As a result, we strongly encourage aspiring P-12 budget managers to identify who they can consult with when they have questions concerning the management of a P-12 budget. Then, consult with that individual or those individuals as questions arise.

ALIGNMENT

As was discussed earlier in the book, the best P-12 budget managers align all spending decisions with the organization's vision, mission, goals, and strategic plan. Spending patterns should clearly demonstrate the values of the organization. Failure to achieve alignment results in greater inefficiency and in ineffective spending decisions. Ultimately, the failure to achieve alignment results in inferior educational opportunities for students within the organization.

TRANSPARENCY

P-12 budget managers should strive to make all money-related decisions in a transparent manner. Transparency fosters greater trust within all individuals in the organization, whereas a lack of transparency garners mistrust and apprehension. P-12 budget managers that master transparency will observe, in addition to greater trust, a greater willingness for cooperation from those within the organization. Transparency is an essential component to collaborative leadership.

COLLABORATE

Budget decisions should, for the most part, be made collaboratively. Educational leaders that fail to collaboratively involve others within the organization in budget decisions unintentionally jeopardize trust between the administration and the staff. Conversely, educational leaders that utilize a building or school district leadership team to make budgetary decisions increase the transparency around financial decisions, augment cooperation for the direction of the organization, and ensure the fiscal decisions align with the desires of the majority of the staff members.

EDUCATE OTHERS

Educational leaders with an expertise in budget management have a responsibility to educate other stakeholders on all aspects of school finance and budgeting. For example, parents (the greatest advocacy group for public education) must understand the strains on the total program for the school or school district and the need for additional funding. Faculty and staff should understand how money and full-time equivalencies flow to school districts and to the individual schools. There are too many P-12 educational leaders that seem to personify the "I don't really know much about finance or budgeting" attitude, and this apathy harms public education. Our hope is that those who read this book will have the knowledge necessary to explain finance and budget concepts and seek out opportunities to do so.

USE KNOWLEDGE TO INFLUENCE OTHERS

Finally, we hope that this book has provided readers with the knowledge of finance and budget that will empower them to influence others. Specifically, public education desperately needs more advocates with a working understanding of financial and budgetary practices that can coherently convince state policymakers to provide public education with adequate funding.

We hope you have discovered the joy associated with effectively managing public funds in a way that maximizes the educational opportunities of each and every student within an organization. A strong understanding of budget-ary practices is imperative for educational leaders seeking to promote greater educational achievement. We feel the content and exercises embedded in this book have provided the reader with the foundation necessary to maximize the power of each public dollar entrusted to P-12 budget managers. We look forward to hearing from readers on how the book has contributed to their abilities to effectively lead schools and school districts.

References

Alexander, K., & R. G. Salmon. 1995. *Public School Finance*. Boston: Allyn and Bacon.

Archibald, R., & D. Feldman. 2006. State higher education spending and the tax revolt. *The Journal of Higher Education, 77* (4), 618–43.

Archibald, R., & D. Feldman. 2008. Explaining increases in higher education costs. *The Journal of Higher Education, 79* (3), 268–95.

Archibald, R., & D. Feldman. 2011. *Why Does College Cost So Much?* New York: Oxford University Press.

Barr, M., & G. McClellan. 2011. *Budgeting and Financial Management in Higher Education*. San Francisco, CA: Jossey-Bass.

Bogaty, E., & J. Nelson. 2013. *Announcement: Moody's: 2013 Outlook for Entire US Higher Education Sector Changed to Negative*. New York, NY: Moody's Investor Services: Global Credit Research.

Box, G., & G. M. Jenkins. 2008. *Time Series Analysis: Forecasting and Control*. Hoboken, NJ: John Wiley & Sons, Inc.

Brimley, Jr., V., D. A. Verstegen, & R. R. Garfield. 2012. *Financing Education in a Climate of Change* (11th ed.). Boston, MA: Pearson.

Chabotar, K. J. 1989. Financial ratio analysis comes to non-profits. *The Journal of Higher Education, 60* (2), 188–208.

Cheslock, J., & M. Gianneschi. 2008. Replacing state appropriations with alternative revenue sources: The case of voluntary support. *The Journal of Higher Education, 79* (2), 208–29.

Coleman, J. S., E. Q. Campbell, C. J. Hobson, J. McPartland, A. M. Mood, F. D. Weinfeld, & R. L. York. 1966. *Equity of Educational Opportunities*. Washington, DC: U.S. Government Printing Office.

Cox, B., S. C. Weiler, & L. M. Cornelius. 2013. *The Costs of Education: Revenues and Spending in Public, Private and Charter Schools*. Lancaster, PA: Pro>Active Publications.

Daley, R. A. 2010. *Determinants of Credit Ratings for US Private Colleges and Universities*, Honors Theses. Paper 576. Retrieved from: http://digitalcommons.colby.edu/honorstheses/576.

Damodaran, A. 2001. *Corporate Finance: Theory and Practice* (2nd ed.). New York, NY: John Wiley & Sons, Inc.

Damodaran, A. 2012. *Investment Analysis: Tools and Techniques for Determining the Value of Any Asset* (3rd ed.). New York, NY: Wiley.

Doty, R. 2012. *Bloomberg Visual Guide to Municipal Bonds*. Hoboken, NJ: Bloomberg Press.

Dunn, W. N. 2012. *Public Policy Analysis* (5th ed.). Upper Saddle River, NJ: Pearson.

Earthman, G. I. (2009). *Planning Educational Facilities* (3rd ed.). New York, NY: Rowman & Littlefield Education.

Ely, T. 2012. Indirect aid for uncertain times: The use of state credit enhancement programs. *Municipal Finance Journal, 33* (2), 61–85.

Feldstein, S., & F. Fabozzi. 2008. *The Handbook of Municipal Bonds*. Hoboken, NJ: John Wiley & Sons, Inc.

Fink, S., & A. Markholt. 2011. *Leading for Instructional Improvement: How Successful Leaders Develop Teaching and Learning Expertise*. San Francisco, CA: Jossey-Bass.

Finkler, S. (2005). *Financial Management for Public, Health, and Not-for-Profit Organizations* (2nd ed.). Upper Saddle River, NJ: Pearson Prentice Hall.

Finkler, S., R. Purtell, T. Calabrese, & D. Smith. (2013). *Financial Management for Public, Health, and Not-for-Profit Organizations* (4th ed). Upper Saddle River, NJ: Pearson.

Fischer, M., Gordon, T. P., Greenlee, J., & Keating, E. K. (2004). Measuring operations: An analysis of US private colleges and universities' financial statements. *Financial Accountability & Management, 20* (2), 129–151.

Goldstein, L. 2012. *A Guide to College & University Budgeting: Foundations for Institutional Effectiveness* (4th ed.). Washington, DC: National Association of College and University Budget Officers.

Governmental Accounting Standards Board. 2006. The user's perspective. *Financial Statement Users*. Retrieved from: http://gasb.org/cs/ContentServer?c=GA SBContent_C&pagename=GASB%2FGASBContent_C%2FUsersArticlePage& cid=1176156737123.

Hanushek, E. A. 1989. The impact of differential expenditures on school performance. *Educational Researcher, 18* (4), 45–65.

Hedges, L. V., R. D. Laine, & R. Greenweld. 1994. An exchange: Part 1: Does money matter? A meta-analysis of studies of the effects of differential school inputs on student outcomes. *Educational Researcher, 23* (3), 5–14.

Hegar, G. 2015. Liabilities payable from restricted assets. *Reporting Requirements for Fiscal Year 2015: Annual Financial Reports of State Agencies and Universities*. Texas Comptroller of Public Accounts. Retrieved from: https://fmx.cpa.state. tx.us/fmx/pubs/afrrptreq/notes/index.php?menu=1&section=note5&page=liabilit ies_payable.

Heller, D. 2006. State support of higher education: Past, present, and future. In *Privatization and Public Universities*, edited by D. Priest and E. St. John. Bloomington, IN: Indiana University Press.

Heller, D. 2011. Trends in the affordability of public colleges and universities: The contradiction of increasing prices and increasing enrollment. In *The States and*

Public Higher Education Policy: Affordability, Access, and Accountability, edited by Donald Heller. Baltimore, MD: The Johns Hopkins University Press.

Hillman, N., D. Tandberg, & J. P. K. Gross. 2014. Performance funding in higher education: Do financial incentives impact college completions? *The Journal of Higher Education, 85* (6), 826–57.

Jacob, B., B. McCall, & K. Stange. 2013. *College as Country Club: Do Colleges Cater to Students' Preferences for Consumption.* Cambridge, MA: National Bureau of Economic Research.

Kalsbeek, D., & D. Hossler. 2008. Enrollment management a market-center perspective. *College & University, 84* (3), 2–11.

Kirp, D. 2003. *Shakespeare, Einstein & the Bottom Line: The Marketing of Higher Education.* Cambridge, MA: Harvard University Press.

Kosten, L., & C. Lovell. 2011. Academic deans' perspective on the effectiveness of responsibility centered management. In *Integrated Resource and Budget Planning at Colleges and Universities*, edited by C. Rylee (pp. 85–101). Ann Arbor, MI: Society for College and University Planning.

Lee, R. D., R. Johnson, & P. Joyce. 2013. *Public Budgeting Systems* (9th ed.). Burlington, MA: Jones & Bartlett Learning.

Lerner, J., A. Schoar, & J. Wang. 2008. Secrets of the academy: The drivers of university endowment success. *The Journal of Economic Perspectives, 22* (3), 207–22.

Lowry, R. 2001b. The effects of state political interests and campus outputs on public university revenues. *Economics of Education Review, 20*, 105–19.

McKeown-Moak, M. P., & C. Mullin. 2014. *Higher Education Finance Research: Policy, Politics, and Practice.* Charlotte, NC: Information Age Publishing.

McLendon, M. K., J. C. Hearn, & R. Deaton. 2006. Called to account: Analyzing the origins and spread of state performance-accountability policies for higher education. *Educational Evaluation and Policy Analysis, 28* (1), 1–24.

McLendon, M., J. Hearn, & C. Mokher. 2009. Partisans, professionals, and power: The role of political factors in state higher education funding. *The Journal of Higher Education, 80* (6), 686–713.

Mincke, B. 2008. How to analyze higher education bonds. In S. Feldstein, & F. Fabozzi, *The Handbook of Municipal Bonds.* Hoboken, NJ: John Wiley & Sons, Inc.

Moody's. 2013. *US Higher Education Outlook Negative in 2013: Revenue Pressure on All Fronts Intensifies Need to Grapple with Traditional Cost Structure.* New York, NY: Moody's Investor Services.

Murnane, R., & Willett, J. (2011). *Methods Matter: Improving Causal Inference in Educational and Social Science Research.* New York, NY: Oxford University Press.

National Center for Education Statistics (NCES). N.d. *Fast Facts.* Retrieved from: http://nces.ed.gov/fastfacts/display.asp?id=66.

NCES. 2010. *Public Elementary and Secondary Students, Schools, Pupil/Teacher Rations, and Finances, by Type of Locale: 2007–2008 and 2008–2009.* Retrieved from: http://nces.ed.gov/programs/digest/d10/tables/dt10_093.asp.

NCES. 2011. *Revenues and Expenditures for Public Elementary and Secondary Education: School Year 2008–2009 (Fiscal Year 2009).* Retrieved from: http://nces.edu.gov/pubs2011/expenditures/tables/table_01.asp.

National Education Association. 2014. *Ranking of the States 2013 & Estimates of School Statistics 2014.* Retrieved from: http://www.nea.org/assets/docs/NEA-Rankings-and-Estimates-2013-2014.pdf.

O'Hara, N. 2012. *The Fundamentals of Municipal Bonds* (6th ed.). Hoboken, NJ: Securities Industry and Financial Markets Association; John Wiley & Sons, Inc.: Wiley Finance.

O'Loughlin, E. 2012. *How to Draw a Basic Control Chart in Excel 2010.* September 25. Retrieved from: https://www.youtube.com/watch?v=zvp8qmH3Eos (accessed August 10, 2014).

Odden, A. R., & L. O. Picus. 2008. *School Finance: A Policy Perspective* (4th ed.). Boston, MA: McGraw Hill.

Pamley, K., A. Bell, H. L'Orange, & P. Lingenfelter. 2009. *State Budgeting for Higher Education in the United States: As Reported for Fiscal Year 2007.* Boulder, CO: State Higher Education Executive Officers.

Parkin, M. 2010. *Microeconomics* (9th ed). Upper Saddle River, NJ: Prentice Hall.

Poudre School District. N.d. *Mission & Vision.* Retrieved from: https://pga.psd-schools.org/about-pga/mission-vision.

Prager, McCarthy, & Sealy. 2002. *Ratio Analysis in Higher Education: New Insights for Leaders of Public Higher Education* (5th ed.). Amstelveen: KPMG LLP.

Rylee, C. 2011. Introduction and overview. In *Integrated Budgeting and Planning at Colleges and Universities*, edited by C. Rylee (p. 1). Ann Arbor, MI: Society for College and University Planning.

SAS/STAT (R). 2009. User's guide. *Mean Squared Error.* SAS Institute, Inc. Retrieved from: http://support.sas.com/documentation/cdl/en/statug/63033/HTML/default/viewer.htm#statug_intromod_sect005.htm (accessed August 6, 2014).

Serna, G. 2013a. Understanding the effects of state oversight and fiscal policy on university revenues: Considerations for financial planning. *Planning for Higher Education, 41* (2), 1–16.

Serna, G. R. 2013b. Employing college and university credit ratings as indicators of institutional planning effectiveness. *Planning for Higher Education, 41* (4), 1–11.

Serna, G. R. 2015. Do tax revolt provisions influence tuition and fee levels? Evidence from the states using recent panel data. *Journal of Education Finance, 41* (1), 48–82.

Serna, G., & S. C. Weiler. 2014. State of the states update: Colorado. *Journal of Education Finance, 39* (3), 250–52.

St. John, E., & D. Priest. 2006. Privatization in public universities. In *Privatization and Public Universities*, edited by D. Priest and E. St. John. Bloomington, IN: Indiana University Press.

Standard & Poor's. 2013. *U.S. Higher Education Sector Could Experience a Rise in Rating and Outlook Changes in 2013.* San Francisco, CA: Standard & Poor's Rating Services: Ratings Direct.

Stevenson, W. 2015. *Operations Management* (12th ed.). New York: McGraw-Hill.

Tandberg, D. 2008. The politics of higher education funding. *Higher Education in Review, 5,* 1–36.

Tandberg, D., & N. Hillman. 2014. State higher education performance funding: Data, outcomes, and policy implications. *Journal of Education Finance, 39* (3), 222–43.

Terenzini, P. Winter 1999. On the nature of institutional research and the knowledge and skills it requires. *New Directions in Institutional Research, 104*, 21–9.

Thelin, J. 2004. Higher education and the public trough. In *Public Funding of Higher Education: Changing Contexts and New Rationales*, edited by Edward St. John and Michael Parsons. Baltimore, MC: The Johns Hopkins University Press.

Toutkoushian, R. 2001. Trends in revenues and expenditures for public and private universities. In *The Finance of Higher Education: Theory, Research, Policy & Practice*, edited by M. Paulsen and J. Smart, (pp. 11–38). New York, NY: Agathon Press.

Toutkoushian, R. 2003. Weathering the storm: Generating revenues for higher education during a recession. In *Maximizing Revenue for Higher Education*, edited by F. Alexander and R. Ehrenberg (pp. 27–40). San Francisco, CA: Josey-Bass.

Trochim, W., & J. Donnelly. 2007. *The Research Methods Knowledge Base* (3rd ed.). Boston, MA: Cengage.

Varlotta, L. 2010. Becoming a leader in university budgeting. In *Student Affairs Budgeting and Financial Management in the Midst of Financial Crisis*, edited by L. Varlotta and B. Jones (pp. 5–20). Hoboken, NJ: Josey-Bass: An Imprint of Wiley.

Vernier: Tech Info Library. 2011. *What Are Mean Squared Error and Root Mean Squared Error?* October 18. Retrieved from: http://www.vernier.com/til/1014/ (accessed August 6, 2014).

Weyl, S., & R. Rodgers. 2006. *Tax-Exempt Bonds: Considerations for College and University Counsel*. Washington, DC: National Association of College and University Attorneys.

Whitehead, B. M., F. Boschee, & R. H. Decker. 2013. *The Principal: Leadership for a Global Society*. Los Angeles, CA: Sage.

Winston, G. 1999. Subsidies, hierarchy and peers: The awkward economics of higher education. *Journal of Economic Perspectives, 13* (1), 13–36.

Yukl, G. 2002. *Leadership in Organizations* (5th ed.). Upper Saddle River, NJ: Prentice Hall.

About the Authors

Spencer C. Weiler, PhD, worked in public education as both a history teacher and an assistant principal in Utah and Virginia for 15 years. After completing his doctoral studies at Virginia Tech with an emphasis on school finance and school law, Dr. Weiler came to the University of Northern Colorado in 2007. Although Dr. Weiler genuinely misses the energy and enthusiasm unique to public schools and working directly with students, he is honored to instill in aspiring educational leaders an understanding of school finance and budget processes. Dr. Weiler strives to use his research to ensure that all students have an appropriate access to education. He has coauthored one book and authored seven book chapters and over fifteen journal articles in the following journals: *Journal of Education Finance*, *Brigham Young University Education Law Journal*, *Educational Considerations*, *Journal of International Education and Leadership*, *Equity and Excellence in Education*, *Planning and Change*, and *West's Education Law Reporter*.

Gabriel R. Serna, PhD, has nearly 13 years of experience in higher education, including as director of programming at New Mexico State University, as assistant director of admissions at the University of Kentucky, as associate instructor at Indiana University Bloomington, as assistant professor in the Higher Education and Student Affairs Leadership program at the University of Northern Colorado, and currently as assistant professor in the School of Education at Virginia Tech. Dr. Serna's research interests lie in the areas of higher education economics, finance, and policy. He is particularly interested in the economic relationships between states and their public institutions, student price-response, college and university fiscal administration, and enrollment management. Some of his published work can be seen in the *Journal of Education Finance*, the *Journal of Higher Education Management*, the *Planning for Higher Education Journal, The Handbook of Strategic Enrollment Management,* and the *Encyclopedia of Education Economics & Finance.* Additionally, Dr. Serna's research was nationally recognized by the *Journal of Education Finance* and the National Education Finance Academy with the "Outstanding Article of the Year" award in 2015.

Made in the USA
San Bernardino, CA
05 May 2018